TRISHA LEIGH SHUFELT

the EVERGLOW

A DIVINATION SYSTEM

REDFeather™

MIND | BODY | SPIRIT

Library of Congress Control Number: 2022932583

Designed by Brenda McCallum
Type set in Gill Sans/ Mailart Rubberstamp

ISBN: 978-0-7643-6504-1
Printed in China

Published by REDFeather Mind, Body, Spirit
An imprint of Schiffer Publishing, Ltd.
4880 Lower Valley Road
Atglen, PA 19310
Phone: (610) 593-1777; Fax: (610) 593-2002
Email: Info@redfeathermbs.com
Web: www.redfeathermbs.com

*To my son, Patrick.
Don't forget to go outside and get some fresh air.
Love, Mom.*

ACKNOWLEDGMENTS

A big thank-you to everyone at Schiffer,
REDFeather, and especially my editor
Peggy Kellar—there isn't a well deep enough to
express my gratitude for you. Thank you to
everyone who continues to support my work
as an artist and writer. I am truly grateful.

CONTENTS

WELCOME

We are always connected to the Earth and it to us. Everything we do repercusses upon it, and everything within it repercusses on us. Unfortunately, most choose to ignore it or are unable to recognize it. The saddest part is that when we fail to reverence any aspect of nature and our intimate connection to it, we are failing to reverence intimate aspects of our own self.

—*Animal Speak* by Ted Andrews

I began creating *The Everglow* shortly after the completion of *The Poe Tarot.* Having spent the better part of two years working on black-and-white images, I longed for color and nature. Like many people locked down during the 2020–21 pandemic, I was limited in my outings and wanted to bring the outside into my art. And, like many, I went inward, looking for answers and guidance. I have always considered myself a spiritual person. In fact, I believe one of my first "ah-ha" moments occurred when watching Obi-Wan Kenobi explain the force to Luke in *Star Wars.* Even at seven years old, I understood what he meant and found that I, too, could sense energy in everything. Perhaps not so esoteric to the legions of fans, but to me it was an epiphany, which set me on the course of my spiritual awakening. Later in life, I would study Reiki and become a master practitioner. Long before my certification, I would spend over thirty years studying various spiritual paths, religions, the Tarot, astrology, etc., much of which I have incorporated into paintings, writing, and, last but not least, my card decks. Still, I am no expert and feel much of my understanding of this human existence is through pure observation, introspection, intuition, and the innate knowing that we all are a part of something greater than ourselves. I'll never be finished trying to figure it all out, and I feel that is why many of us are always searching for our soul's path. Perhaps that is why I began designing oracle and Tarot decks. The quote above by the late Ted Andrews has guided the inspiration of *The Everglow* in particular. After all, nature is the essence of all creativity, and our connection to nature is the essence of our planet's survival. While I am an artist by trade, I am a nomad under the skin. *The Everglow* is a culmination of all the roads less traveled. I hope it opens gateways leading to the introspection of profound answers, and those answers lead to more questions that will provide magic along the way.

INTRODUCTION

The Everglow is a beautifully illustrated deck featuring animal images and humanlike people interacting with nature. It's a unique system incorporating elements of the Tarot and oracle while exploring aspects of numerology, animal symbolism, and astrology. Providing various options for reading, which will be discussed further in the guidebook, *The Everglow*'s fantastical montage of images focuses on our universal connection and interdependence on each other in these challenging times. While there are animals and a nice balance between human faces and races depicting feminine and masculine images, their presence is not meant to force focus on any specific gender, race, or animal. Instead, I hope the reader will see themselves within these characters and move fluidly within their roles. Interdependence creates similarity. Where there is difference, there is also unity. Whether we look into human or animal eyes, we have the opportunity to experience the ancient wisdom of the soul, and from there, we may hear the message of our connectedness.

A BRIEF OVERVIEW OF THE TAROT

While *The Everglow* is its own system, you will notice that it has many similarities to a Tarot deck. I'm assuming that if you have purchased this deck, you may already be familiar with the Tarot; however, if you are not, I will provide a brief overview. I say brief because there are hundreds of books on the Tarot, and they are all different in some respect.

The Tarot has been around since the fifteenth century and was used throughout Europe primarily as a card game. It wasn't until the eighteenth century that it was more widely used for "occult" purposes. Simply put, the Tarot is a tool for divination. *Merriam-Webster defines divination as the art or practice that seeks to foresee or foretell future events or discover hidden knowledge, usually by the interpretation of omens or by the aid of supernatural powers.* Sounds spooky and otherworldly, doesn't it? Perhaps this is just one of the reasons why the Tarot has been so maligned. I personally like the word "cartomancy," which is also known as fortune-telling and divination, but it has a lovelier ring to the ear. Some use the Tarot to predict future events. I feel that its use for divining intuition to seek answers from within is universal, and therefore, anyone can learn and benefit from the Tarot. While the interpretation of the Tarot and its symbols may be personal and varied, the one thing that is the same is the structure of the Tarot—seventy-eight cards that include a Major and Minor Arcana.

Now that I have given you a brief history of the Tarot, let's discuss how *The Everglow*'s Arcana is similar and different from the Major Arcana in the Tarot.

ARCANA COMPARISONS

The Tarot consists of seventy-eight cards, as does *The Everglow*. The first twenty-two cards in the Tarot are called the Major Arcana. We will discuss these cards here, and the remaining fifty-six cards in detail later in the book.

In Tarot, the Major Arcana follows the Fool's Journey from 0 to 21. Those twenty-two cards have names, such as the Fool, the Magician, the Hanged Man, etc. Each card depicts images rich in symbolism, which feature lessons through archetypal themes significantly impacting your life's journey. Archetypes are people or relatable personality traits, and these cards are essential because when they show up in a reading, matters of fate and opportunities for spiritual growth are prevalent.

The Everglow Arcana includes these twenty-two cards, but instead of an archetype title on each card, keywords incorporating the card's overall meaning are given. These keywords were derived from an extensive study into the traditional themes of each card in the Tarot. *The Everglow* Arcana has two words on each card. The left word represents the card when read in the upright position, and the right word describes it in the reversed position. Many practitioners read reversals, and therefore I felt it essential to include them in this deck; however, incorporating them in your readings is a matter of choice. All seventy-eight cards in *The Everglow* deck have keywords, thus allowing it to function as an oracle, which is part of the system's beauty. As mentioned earlier, *The Everglow* features animals as well as humans. Where there are animals, I will speak a bit about their symbolism when discussing those cards. Below is a list of *The Everglow* Arcana cards and the corresponding traditional Tarot card title. These cards are numbered like traditional Tarot to showcase their significance in any given reading. In discussing each *Everglow* card's meaning, I will reflect upon the Tarot from time to time but will not provide specific Tarot card meanings. However, rest assured that each card within *The Everglow* was influenced by the traditional Rider-Waite-Smith system.

the EVERGLOW   TAROT

0.	Opportunity/Risk	Fool
1.	Manifestation/Focus	Magician
2.	Intuition/Bias	High Priestess
3.	Abundance/Self-Care	Empress
4.	Foundation/Control	Emperor
5.	Guidance / Inner Wisdom	Hierophant
6.	Alignment/Disharmony	Lovers
7.	Determination/Obstacles	Chariot
8.	Challenges / Inner Strength	Strength
9.	Introspection/Isolation	Hermit
10.	Movement/Patterns	Wheel of Fortune
11.	Cause/Effect	Justice
12.	Surrender/Resistance	Hanged Man
13.	Transformation/Stagnation	Death
14.	Moderation/Extremism	Temperance
15.	Shadow/Confrontation	Devil
16.	Upheaval/Awakening	Tower
17.	Hope/Despair	Star
18.	Projections/Clarity	Moon
19.	Optimism/Pessimism	Sun
20.	Calling/Shrink	Judgment
21.	Attainment/Time	World

ANIMAL SYMBOLISM

Before getting into an explanation about each card in *The Everglow* Arcana, I want to make a quick mention of animal symbolism and why it is crucial to this deck. When I began creating *The Everglow*, I intended to create a deck featuring only animals; however, as it evolved, I felt the interaction between animals and humans was an essential texture in the deck. After all, humans would utilize the deck, and the connection between animals and humans is paramount in the age of climate change. Let's face it, many of us live in neighborhoods lacking a connection to nature other than birds. I lived for many years in a suburban area that saw little to no wildlife until I moved to my new home, which sits near the woods. The first time I saw a bear and later a bobcat in my yard was a real shock to my senses. While my house was on the land, the woods belonged to them, and we were going to have to share the space between us. I had to honor and respect their presence.

I mention Ted Andrews's book *Animal Speak* in the foreword as one of the inspirations for *The Everglow*. In chapter I, he says:

> In the past shamans, priests, and priestesses were the keepers of the sacred knowledge of life. These individuals were tied to the rhythms and forces of nature. They were capable of walking the threads that link the invisible and visible worlds. They helped people remember that all trees are divine and that all animals speak to those who listen.

He further says:

The early priest/ess-magicians would adopt the guise of animals—wearing skins and masks to symbolize a reawakening and endowing of oneself with specific energies.

The majority of humans / humanlike characters in *The Everglow* were designed to look otherworldly, as though they were the priests, priestesses, shamans, and magicians of the past that Mr. Andrews references. In this deck, they are no wiser than their animal companions—they are merely interpreters of the wisdom the animal wishes to impart.

ANIMAL ASSOCIATIONS

Birds and air creatures symbolize a connection to the Divine. They serve to awaken our links among the earth, our soul, and the higher realms. They inspire us in our creativity, help us overcome great odds, allow us to soar to new heights, and communicate ancient wisdom.

Water creatures encourage us to explore more profound emotional matters, the subconscious realms, inner guidance, and imagination.

Earth creatures root and ground us. The earth is where seeds are planted and things grow; thus, they symbolize ideas into manifestation—stability, security, growth, strength, hard work, and foundation.

Fire creatures symbolize our passion and regenerative abilities.

the EVERGLOW

ARCANA IMAGES AND INTERPRETATIONS

The Rabbit stands on the precipice of a large green hill as the sun shines brightly behind him, contemplating a leap into the unknown. He is alert, possibly a bit pensive, but excited and curious about where this leap of faith will take him. After a moment, he bursts forth with an open mind and trusts that all will be well.

Like the Fool in Tarot, this card alerts you of opportunities to experience bright new beginnings. While it is normal to feel apprehensive when embarking on new possibilities, you are encouraged to release your fears and trust the process. This is a time of personal growth. Embrace the unknown with enthusiasm.

Reversed~ You may be feeling anxious and fearful. Perhaps you think you need more time or don't have all the information necessary to move forward. This is all perfectly natural. Any new opportunity is not without risk and concern. However, now is the time to go within to calm your inner voice. If you feel the need for caution, by all means take your time but do not miss out on an opportunity because of fear. Remember the difference between genuine fear, which you sense when you are in harm's way, and false fear, which appears real but lacks merit and typically stems from imprints, previous experiences, or bias.

SYMBOL

Rabbit~ "Rabbit. Rabbit. Rabbit." How many times have you said this at the beginning of a new month before uttering another word? Many do so for luck because they see a new month as a fresh start. The rabbit is more than a cute and fluffy creature. It is rich in symbolism. Think abundance, growth potential, and creation. The rabbit is also keenly sensitive to its environment and, while playful, always keeps a watchful eye on danger. They are associated with spring, a time of new buds bursting forth from the ground and a time when rabbits are particularly procreative. Rabbits burrow underground, and this earthly connection reminds us of a need to ground and center when we feel anxious about the unknown. While at times appearing timid, the rabbit is not afraid to stand up to predators and never lets fear hold it back from exploration.

An elegant spider weaves a web between two trees while the sun rises and sets behind her. If she stays focused on the end result, she knows she will achieve her goal. Similar to the Magician in the Tarot, the spider is the ultimate alchemist, drawing upon the tools within to manifest her dreams, not just through thought but also through dedicated action. She also knows that the magic of manifestation occurs when we believe we are worthy of receiving. Now is the time to believe in yourself and put forth your skills toward a desired goal.

Reversed~ Hesitation could be causing you to lose focus on the prize. Perhaps you are trying too hard to control the outcome, and a bit of flexibility is required. Sometimes, we miss opportunities because we fear we lack what it takes or simply do not deserve the reward. On other occasions, we may be quick to rush an outcome and become displeased with the time it takes to see progress or the end result. Now is not the time to cut corners. Remember, everything in Divine timing.

SYMBOLS

Spider/Web~ The spider represents feminine energy. Just like the Magician who utilizes tools from within to manifest an outcome, the spider is the ultimate symbol of creation through the intricate webs she weaves. She draws forth from her own body to create a masterpiece and then sits back to await her prize. It takes time and patience, which she has in abundance. She knows that anything worth achieving is worth waiting for, but she also knows she must put forth the effort. Nothing will come by merely wishing it into being. Spiders are feared by some, and because of this, she calls into question the fears that may be preventing you from manifesting what you truly deserve. Fear is often what prevents us from achieving a goal or a dream, because we know our circumstances may change once we step on the path. Change brings about the unknown. I am reminded of the quote by Erin Hanson: "There is freedom waiting for you, on the breezes of the sky, and you ask, 'What if I fall?' Oh, but my darling, What if you fly?"

A beautiful woman sits against the backdrop of a glowing full moon. She looks deep within your eyes and, without words, offers ancient wisdom discovered only from within the hidden realms. The shadowy blackbird accompanying her allows her to fly effortlessly between the conscious and subconscious realms to deliver these messages. She is the embodiment of Divine knowledge, and she resides within all of us. She calls on you to connect with her through your intuition to uncover the secrets within your soul. Furthermore, she is the bridge between the feminine and masculine, which we all embody. She brings forth balance between the two and, in doing so, deepens our empathy and compassion toward ourselves and the outside world.

All answers are found within, but we must learn to connect with our intuitive nature to discover them. We can do this in various ways, such as meditation, journaling, quiet reflection, dreams, and the arts.

Reversed~ You are having a difficult time connecting to your intuition, and it could be because your own bias is getting in the way. Bias occurs when we allow judgment to cloud our thinking. This could be because we are putting too much value into others' thoughts and beliefs, stifling our intuitive feelings. Perhaps old patterns, fears, and imprints are also clouding our intuition. Now is the time to quiet the mind and block out anything extraneous that prevents you from connecting with your inner knowing.

SYMBOLS

Blackbird/Crow/Raven~ I use the term "blackbird" when describing this card, but you could connect with crow and raven energy as well. All three are known messengers from the hidden realms. The raven and crow, in particular, are brilliant birds with multiple communication capabilities. Full moons are connected with our emotions and feelings and may bring forth dreams that provide messages from the subconscious realms. The waning moon upon the priestesses' forehead reminds us to slow down and turn inward and to do so consciously and without judgment.

The beekeeper woman is the embodiment of the Empress energy found in the Tarot. She sits in impending motherhood and is surrounded by an abundance of flowers as she feeds her honeybees from the hive upon her head. A crow envelopes her with his massive wings in protection. She exudes feminine energy and creative endeavors through the fullness of her belly. The beehive is her homage to the natural earthly realms, while the crow connects her to the Divine mysteries of the universe. In the upright position, she reminds you that you are surrounded by abundance and beauty. You have everything you need, and if there is something you wish to achieve, know it will occur after a period of gestation. The end result will be exactly what you need when you need it.

Reversed~ Time to self-nurture. You may have been giving too much to others and neglecting your own needs—time to get out in nature or go inward with some pampering. If there is something you wish to create but are finding it difficult, now is the time to examine what is standing in your way. Is it others, control issues, or self-talk keeping you from your goal? For now, take some time to create for creation's sake without any attachments regarding the outcome.

SYMBOLS

Crow~ Transformation, change, and protection

Bee~ Harmony, family, and nurturing

Hive~ Home, comfort, and security

Flowers~ Abundance, growth, and beauty

In this image, we see a ram-horned man with the sun shining brightly behind him. He stands behind two of his flock, with hands placed on their backs as he looks out toward the future. Standing in authority, he is equivalent to the Emperor in Tarot, and his main goal is building solid foundations. He is trusted, fair, nonjudgmental, and full of passion, power, and wisdom. He is also not afraid of hard work and perseverance. No matter what gender you identify with, this card suggests you are taking on a position of authority or control. You are building solid foundations or may be relied on by others because they see you as a pillar of strength. You are drawing on your experience, tools, and knowledge to build better security or find that others seek you out because of your expertise.

Reversed~ While it's important to step into our sense of power, we mustn't get carried away by utilizing it in harmful, manipulative, or overly controlling ways, since this will leave others around us feeling powerless. Equally, if we are shrinking from our power due to insecurity, fear, or perhaps giving our power away, it's time to examine why. You may need to exert your independence if you are relying on others to build solid foundations for you.

SYMBOLS

Ram~ Determination, power, protection, leadership, and strength. Stubbornness and hostility are other traits of ram energy when put to negative use. Rams are a key symbol for the Emperor in the traditional Rider-Waite-Smith deck.

This may be a time when you are seeking answers or further knowledge from sources outside yourself. In doing so, you may find it helpful to follow tried-and-tested models to rectify or better certain situations. Perhaps you are seeking like-minded individuals whose perspectives and experiences are comforting. Knowledge is power.

Reversed~ Take a deep breath. Breathe out. Do this a few more times. Ahhh, there it is—listen. Sometimes all we need is a quiet moment of contemplation to hear the wisdom of our inner voice. After all, we can be our own best teachers through our built-in guidance system. While there are times when we need to seek advice from others, sometimes we may find the answers we are seeking have been there all along, but we failed to hear them because we simply weren't tuning out the extraneous.

SYMBOLS

Feathers~ Divine guidance, angelic realms, angels, healing, messages, bridge connection between the earth and the spirit realms, blessings, and accession

In the Tarot, this card is represented as the Lovers card. Although it can be indicative of a loving partnership, it is also about a variety of relationships. We have so many throughout our lifetime, and each one is a moment for teaching and learning. The most important relationship we have is with ourselves. The Lovers card is also about choices that change our course or path in life. It's essential to note that swans do not fly but, rather, float along the water, and, in doing so, they remind us of the importance of being at peace or going with the flow of life. Sometimes, that is a choice as well.

 Disharmony in a relationship can occur due to several factors. This may be an important time to examine give and take within the partnership, boundaries, codependencies, and feelings (i.e., how emotionally involved the individuals are). This does not have to pertain to love. It may have to do with business partners as well. Again, essential choices may need to be made, or at the very least, important conversations should be had. Since we have a relationship with ourselves, you may wish to ask, What do I need to feel harmony?

SYMBOLS

Swans~ Love, beauty, romance, purity, loss, persistence, and perseverance

Our sailor sets his course. His ship is strong, and his will is mighty. He has weathered many storms and draws upon previous knowledge to guide his way. Even if you encounter challenges along the way, nothing is out of reach when you harness your will-power and focus on your goals. Keep forging ahead. Success is imminent.

Reversed~ Now is the time to examine what obstacles are keeping you from your desired goals. Are they tangible, or is there something else going on that is keeping you from moving forward? Have you lost your enthusiasm for what you are doing? Are you concerned about what will happen once you reach your desired goal? What will change? Or is this simply a time to course-correct and change your direction? Take a moment to look at what you want before moving forward. Sometimes the reverse of this card can signal a need to loosen up the reigns a bit. We can't always control everything, and doing so can make things seem out of control. Relax your hold and see where the current takes you. You might be pleasantly surprised.

SYMBOLS

Coral~ Change and hard work

Nautilus~ Patterns, rebirth, sacred geometry, strength, going within, and growth among challenges

Koi~ According to Chinese legend, the Dragon's Gate is located at the top of a waterfall. Many koi will swim upstream against the river's strong current to dramatically leap over the waterfall. Few are able to do so. Those that do are transformed into powerful dragons. Now is the time for perseverance and courage. Unleash your inner dragon.

Water~ Emotions, currents, energy, flow, and subconscious

Little fox sits quietly, listening to her inner wisdom. She draws upon her strength, knowing she has weathered many storms, and should another come her way, she will do so with grace. Unlike card number 7, which focuses on outer courage to overcome obstacles, this card is all about harnessing inner strength to deal with difficult situations. I want you to take a moment and look back on past difficulties and how you found the courage to get through those situations. What did it teach you? Did you learn to trust? Did you learn the difference between real and perceived fear? Looking back can often help redirect our knee-jerk, initial reactions, which can often do us more harm than good. Approaching the situation by asking what can this teach me often redirects the energy and the outcome.

Reversed~ Now is the time to check in with yourself to examine what is depleting your resources. Something may be throwing you out of balance. Take some time for self-care. Emotions are good indicators of what needs healing.

SYMBOLS

Fox~ Cleverness, resourcefulness, playfulness, and adaptability

Snow~ Hardship. Melting snow can indicate the end of hardship. Divine voice. Individuality. Gentleness and silence.

Mountain/Hill~ Challenges, obstacles, hard work, goal, step by step, tasks, peak, uphill battle, downhill from here, and success

Pine Tree~ Longevity, peace, sustainability, survival, strength. Cones from a pine tree represent renewal.

This card is represented by the Hermit in the Tarot. As a reader and card designer, I often like to see which direction the Hermit is facing. Even more important, I look at the direction the Hermit faces concerning the cards surrounding it. In this card's design, I purposely made *The Everglow*'s Hermit a fairy with her back to the reader. She is facing neither left nor right but rather going inward or looking outward, depending on your perspective in the situation. She sits in front of a full moon, unencumbered and free. Is the light coming from the moon or from our little fae? Now is the time for deep introspection. You may be at a crossroads and need time to reflect on how you arrived where you are on your journey. Take some time to go within to see if you are heading in the right direction or if you would like to change course. Perhaps you are on a spiritual journey of self-discovery.

Reversed~ The reverse of this card could indicate you are too caught up in the mundane of life and are neglecting your spirit. Something is out of balance, making it difficult for you to hear what you need or what is necessary. Take some time out to breathe, reflect, and listen. All answers are found within. Sometimes, this card's extreme can indicate you are isolating too much and need to connect with others. Don't be afraid to reach out.

SYMBOLS

Moon~ Illumination, cycles, emptying out, completion, and clarity

Fairy~ Ability to move between realms, playfulness, shyness, contradiction, magic, imagination, and riddles

Our sweet seahorse represents the Wheel in the Tarot. He's on a journey and is carrying with him a tiny nautilus shell. This card represents our karmic journey. No two paths are the same, and everyone's path is a series of cycles and destinations. Life is in flux, and so are we. When this card is in the upright position, it indicates things are moving in your favor or, at the very least, forward. Be aware that what goes around does indeed come around, and within every pattern is a lesson learned.

Reversed~ Things may seem out of control, or an unexpected change or setback may have come your way. This is a chance to regain your control. Ask yourself how you got here. Is there anything that has brought you to this moment? Is there anything you are resisting?

SYMBOLS

Seahorse~ Patience, commitment, uniqueness, inflexibility, protection, luck, good fortune, and stubbornness

Shell/Nautilus~ Patterns, rebirth, sacred geometry, strength, going within, and growth among challenges

Mother bird is none too happy about the intruder to her nest. She is fiercely protective of what is hers, and is not afraid of punishing those who wish to cause her eggs harm. While this image is pretty dire, it is a reminder to remember that every action in life has consequences. Be aware of the choices you make, since they may affect others. While there are two sides to every story, and the truth is somewhere in the middle, your actions may be called into question. If you have done nothing wrong, then you will likely receive a fair judgment. However, if you have done something wrong, it may be time to face the consequences of those actions. Typically, when this card is in the upright position, things will be ruled in your favor.

Reversed~ You have done something wrong, and now it is time to own up to your mistake. Hiding it isn't going to make it go away. There is balance in everything. Some consequences must be faced. Face them and move forward.

SYMBOLS

Snake~ Balance, duality, femininity, rebirth, magic, transformation, and cunning

Eggs~ Fertility, rebirth, possibility, manifestation, life, and mystery

Nest~ Home, luck, prosperity, health, happiness, stability, growth, karma. A nest found on your property is a symbol of luck, harmony, and prosperity for all who dwell there.

Black Bird / Crow / Raven~ Messengers, mystery, change, shift, and temptation. These birds are often seen as negative, but I believe they offer more positive rather than negative symbolism. Their color alone speaks to the idea that all answers are found within.

I have never looked at the traditional image of the Hanged Man in the Tarot and not thought of a chrysalis. When this card appears, it reminds you that things are going on beneath the surface that we may not be aware of, and that they are for our best and highest good. Sometimes one needs to surrender to the process to be transformed. Other times, we need to release what no longer serves us, to open ourselves to new opportunities. We may need to make a voluntary retreat or pause, while at other times it is beyond our control. The old adage of making time for yourself or otherwise it will be made for you may apply.

Reversed~ You may be resisting what is evident and will be forced to accept the consequences of those actions. For example, you may need to deal with something but find it easier to avoid it altogether by keeping busy or filling your time with distractions. As they say, what we resist persists. Now is the time to surrender to what needs facing.

SYMBOLS

Chrysalis~ Metamorphosis, growth, transformation, release, shelter, surrender, and awakening

This card symbolizes the end of a major phase in your life and the beginning of something new. We literally see death in a mask guarding her precious eggs, the symbol of rebirth. While this type of transformation can be uncomfortable, it is often needed to usher in something more meaningful and rewarding. Allow it to move through you, letting go of the past, so you may embrace the new. This is a welcome change.

Reversed~ Your life is about to change, but you are resisting it. What is preventing you from this significant transformation? What do you need to release? What fears are you holding on to? Sometimes it feels more comfortable to stay where you are and resist the unknown, but this keeps us stagnant. Now is the time to step into the unknown.

SYMBOLS

Eggs~ Fertility, rebirth, possibility, manifestation, life, and mystery

Nest~ Home, luck, prosperity, health, happiness, stability, growth, karma. A nest found on your property is a symbol of luck, harmony, and prosperity for all who dwell there.

Skull~ Time, power, divinity, transformation, life, and death. The Celts believed the skull was the seat of the soul.

Spiral~ Karma, patterns, consciousness, evolution, creation, surrender, balance, and expansion

Mask~ Concealment, mystery, protection, and secrets

MODERATION / EXTREMISM

Have you heard the old Cherokee legend about the two wolves? In the story, an elderly Cherokee tells his grandson about a battle between two wolves. One is filled with anger, evil, greed, jealousy, and lies, while the other is filled with good, joy, kindness, and humility. He further explains that these wolves are within us all. The grandson looks at him and asks, "Which one will win?" The Cherokee says, "The one that you choose to feed."

I have always loved this parable, and I taught it to my son when he was very young. He still refers to it from time to time. This is what we see in this image.

Two extremes, and somewhere between the two there is balance. Life is a delicate dance, especially in today's society, where it is easy to become "triggered" or reactionary. This is not to say we shouldn't feel our emotions. We definitely should, since it is better to let them out rather than let them rage inside.

This card represents the delicate balance between the two. In the upright position, the card reminds you to keep moderation in mind. Even if life is stressful, it is important to seek balance. You may also find yourself in a situation of opposing forces, and you are the one providing the equilibrium.

Reversed~ Be careful of excessive and extremist behavior. When this card is reversed, it reminds you that something is out of balance, and you are taking things to the extreme. This could be in the form of emotions, spending, or vices. Ask yourself why this is happening. You may need to remove yourself from toxic situations that are only making these behaviors worse.

SYMBOLS

Wolves~ Family, protection, joy, aggression, darkness, and community. Extremes between wealth and poverty.

I've never been a fan of the traditional Devil card in the Tarot, and when I set out to design this card, I knew I wanted something vastly different. The traditional Rider-Waite-Smith card depicts Baphomet, the sabbatic goat, and is derived in part from the image drawn by Éliphas Lévi. In it, the horned creature is atop an altar with two human demons, one male and one female, chained to each other below him. In the image, they appear in a state of bondage, whereby they are becoming more and more like their captor. The irony is they have a choice.

I have always thought of this card as a battle with the self. Therefore, we see our little ying/yang panda confronting his shadow. This card is not just about making change but confronting the shadow existing within us all. Shadow can keep us bound in toxic behaviors, in codependencies, and it can also prevent us from moving forward because of how we see ourselves. When this card is in the upright position, it is time to confront the influences keeping you in a state of bondage. We all have been in situations or relationships that do not serve our best and highest good. We also have the choice to change or leave these toxic situations and people. Ask yourself the hard questions: What or who is holding you back from making the necessary change? Is it you? Often the answer is yes. You are the one who holds the power of change.

Reversed~ You are on the verge of significant change, but to step into your highest potential, you must release anything keeping you in a state of fear and bondage.

SYMBOLS

Panda~ Peace, strength, balance, yin/yang, healthful boundaries, nurture, and polarity

Shadow~ Ego, negative thoughts, inner wisdom, lessons, mystery, subconscious, questions, and access to the light within

This card depicts a tree being struck by lightning while a rabbit eyes the sky of the approaching storm.

Equivalent to the Tower card, when *The Everglow* version appears, great transformation is occurring. You may recall that the number seven in numerology—which is the number sixteen reduced to a single digit—indicates inner and spiritual growth. Nothing could be truer for this card. If you take the one and six and look at them separately, you will further deduce opportunities for new possibilities. Still, often, equilibrium is restored when everything unnecessary is removed. Breakdowns usher in breakthroughs, and this card is all about that process. This quote from the universe, "I had to make you uncomfortable; otherwise, you never would have moved," is very fitting for the upright version of this card. Any Tower moment I have experienced is relatable to that quote. I may not have been able to understand why at the time, but as they say, hindsight is 20/20. In the upright position, the upheaval may come as a shock or surprise that can be uncomfortable and difficult. However, when everything settles, we can look at the events with perspective. The illusions of what we thought were true for us at the time fade, and from new growth there is clarity.

Reversed~ While the upright version points to something out of the blue forcing change, the reversal indicates you are making intentional decisions to change a situation for your best and highest good. This would be a profound transformation resulting from an awakening. Either way, this is a "change" or "be changed" moment.

SYMBOLS

Tree~ Life, self-growth, roots, branching out, discovery, letting go, and weathering the storm

Lightning~ Sign, fear, truth, illumination, power, enlightenment, clarity, and strength

Fire~ Rebirth, resurrection, destruction, bravery, purification, action, and power

Rabbit~ Prosperity, abundance, fear, timid, luck, awareness, rebirth, and growth

Recall the scene in *Harry Potter* when Harry calls upon his Patronus, and a stag appears. The Patronus is described by the wizarding world as an anti-Dementor. Dementors feed upon hope and happiness, while the Patronus is a protector shielding Harry from the Dementor. How fitting that this card, traditionally known. as the Star, should be represented by a stag.

This card appears after you have experienced a profound but challenging transformation. However, what you have endured has provided you with hope and belief that nothing is out of your reach. You are indeed stronger from your experience. You are looking at life with a renewed perspective and feel open to possibility and guidance.

Reversed~ The reverse of this card may have you feeling a sense of despair. Sometimes this is because life can feel overwhelming and complicated. Endless challenges and burdens may have you questioning, "Why me?" Step back for a moment and remember you are not being singled out or punished. Surrendering to the process to understand that something profound can be learned from it often changes the vibration. Whatever the result, be it change or growth, there are lessons indeed learned.

SYMBOL

Stag~ Strength, renewal, rebirth, and protection

Our blackbird now sits perched on a branch, his reflection cast into the waters below by a full moon.

Sometimes, we cannot see things clearly because we project our fear, imprints, and previous experiences onto a particular situation. When this card is drawn, it is an opportunity to step back and examine the problem from a different angle.

Ask yourself some difficult questions.

What emotions are coming up, and why? Do they need clearing? Many of these imprints exist in the subconscious mind and surface when we feel triggered or unsure. While some feelings appear to keep you safe, others can hinder you from moving forward. Be aware of the illusory energy that surrounds the situation.

Reversed~ The reverse of this card indicates clarity. This could be because you are taking a decisive approach to examine the problem with discernment versus emotionally. It also could be that more information is now prevalent, making it easier to see the situation with clarity.

SYMBOLS

Moon~ Illumination, cycles, emptying out, completion, and clarity

Water~ Emotions, currents, energy, flow, secrets, and subconscious

Reflection~ Projections, reflections, internal truth, spirituality, truth, illusion, consequences, awareness, and wisdom

Black Bird / Raven / Crow~ Messengers, mystery, change, shift, and temptation. Their color alone speaks to the idea that all answers are found within.

One of the most optimistic cards in the deck, this card has few if any negative qualities and is represented by the noble horse. When it appears in the upright position, you may be experiencing a feeling of happiness and optimism in your life. Health and vitality are favored. You are radiating a sense of positivity, and others are taking notice. Things are definitely going your way.

Reversed~ Even in the reversed position, this card isn't bad. It is simply a reminder to look on the brighter side of life. You may be letting negative perceptions cloud your feelings. Make some time to play and have fun.

SYMBOLS

Horse~ Power, nobility, strength, freedom, and life-force energy

Sun~ Vitality, life, energy, power, soul, and strength

Little mouse is being called to a higher purpose, but he has a choice to make. Will he rise to his calling or shrink?

Once you set upon the path of your higher calling, there is no turning back. This card appears when you are amid a profound spiritual awakening. You may be seeking something more or making choices aligning with your soul purpose. Now is the time to shed the fears, imprints, and perceptions of the past to see the bigger picture of what lies ahead for you.

Reversed~ Opportunities are being presented, but you may be shrinking from them because of preconceived fears or even "imposter syndrome." Perhaps you are playing it safe, procrastinating, or relying on self-doubt to be your guide. Cast aside the self-talk and step into your power.

SYMBOLS

Sun~ Vitality, life, energy, power, soul, and strength

Mouse~ Ingenuity, resourcefulness, timidness, shyness, awareness, determination, perseverance, purpose, hard work, details, sacrifice, unassuming, and tiny miracles

The oyster must endure the discomfort of a grain of sand to produce the wonder of a pearl. Life can be uncomfortable and challenging. However, it is often the challenges we overcome that produce the most-valuable lessons. When I was diagnosed with breast cancer in 2015, I had trouble seeing ahead. I wasn't sure where the journey would take me, and I knew it would be uncomfortable and challenging. It was all those things and more. But looking back, I've come to realize I was being called to something higher, and I had to answer the call to understand the purpose. In the end, I appreciated the pearl of wisdom created from the journey.

This card appears when you have reached a point of fulfillment, accomplishment, or closure regarding a situation. It is now time to claim your prize or look forward to the next project with hope and enthusiasm.

Reversed~ The reverse of this card may indicate that a bit more time is needed, and now is not the time to throw in the towel. Perhaps a bit more effort and focus are the key to achieving your goal. It could also be that you are seeking closure to something requiring deep introspection and perspective.

SYMBOLS

Oyster~ Birth, hidden treasures, protection, home, sensitivity, sexuality, inner self, harmony, balance, yin/yang (hard outer shell / soft inner belly), duality, strength, struggle to triumph

Pearl~ Prize, reward, gift, overcoming obstacles, overcoming stress, culmination, prosperity, wholeness, moon, wealth, wisdom, purity, and journey of the soul

the EVERGLOW
COURT AND SYMBOLISM

The Everglow Court is unique because instead of having a King, Queen, Knight, and Page representing four different suits, you have just four cards. Regardless, if you draw from these specific cards or mix them in with the other Everglow image cards, it is the individual suit cards (Emotions, Thoughts, Action, or Security) that determine the type of person we are dealing with or the aspect of personality the court card embodies, whether your own or someone else's. While court cards can be associated with specific people, they also speak to particular motivations around forthcoming situations or events. The reversed aspect of a court card is the shadow side of your own character or challenging personalities in others. Either way, when we encounter these people, there are lessons to learn.

Kings and Queens likely represent people you know or aspects of personality versus actual situations. Knights and Pages (the Messenger in *The Everglow*) are doers, movers, and shakers. They more likely represent situations.

If several court cards show up in a reading, it may indicate many people are influencing the situation. If a King or Queen shows up, it's possible you are mastering a particular situation or stepping into your power.

Whether or not you read them as gender specific is purely a matter of choice. Below are a few generalizations to remember about each court card.

KING Organizer, fathers, father figure, boss, leadership role, experience, authority, power position, and maturity. Great organizers and planners.

QUEEN Mothers, mother figures, mature women, authority, power figure, creative, protective, and nurturing. Also, excellent organizers and planners.

KNIGHT Sons, brothers, action, movement, determination, ambition, high energy, restless energy, and active

MESSENGER (PAGE) Sisters, daughters, young, youthful, catalyst for change, communication (written or verbal), im- maturity, and fresh starts

Our King looks like a woodland Santa or forest wizard. His long beard transforms into water, showing he is in touch with his emotional side and shaped by years of wisdom. His eyes are kind but determined. He surrounds himself with various animals, representing a corresponding element, symbolic of the traditional suits in the Tarot that also depict aspects of his personality. The beaver is a family animal and knows the importance of hard work and community. In fact, he is so dedicated to providing a safe environment that he will work tirelessly to achieve his goals. He is resourceful and eager, and deeply connected to water because his emotions are in the heart of everything he does. The noble lion is associated with the element fire because his bright golden mane represents the sun in many cultures. He is the embodiment of strength, courage, and power. The buffalo connects to the earthly realms.

He reminds you to remain grounded and appreciative of the gifts of abundance. He is the consummate symbol of prosperity and security. And finally, the falcon connects us to the air element. Falcon's intense focus and determination mean he knows what he wants and remains on target until he achieves his goal.

Hint~ When the King appears, he is reminding you to step into your power. You are setting up foundations and security for yourself and others. It is also possible you are being influenced or surrounded by someone characteristic of a kingly nature—a fatherly type of person.

Reversed~ Kings in the reversed position represent the more negative aspects of a personality. Arrogant, intolerant, manipulative, self-absorbed, and egotistical are just a few adjectives that describe a reversed King's character. Despite this, should you encounter this type of person, ask yourself how this person's presence in your life can be a teaching tool for growth.

Buffalo~ Strength. Sacred path or journey. Security. Abundance. Gratitude.

Falcon~ Vision. Source connection. Wisdom. Passion. Focus.

Lion~ Family. Courage. Nobility. Honor. Leadership.

Beaver~ Community. Harmony. Hard work. Overcoming obstacles.

The Everglow Queen surrounds herself with many types of creatures and even a few mythical ones as well. She is deeply connected to all realms and shares in their creation. Her eyes depict inner wisdom and ancient knowing that come from experience and her profound intuitive nature. She has a great capacity to love and nurture while providing a safe harbor from the storm. She is changeable and timeless. While our King was surrounded by animals representing the elements of earth, air, fire, and water, she has chosen various creatures within the four seasons.

The rabbit is connected to the earth element and is primal energy. He symbolizes sex, abundance, health, and vitality. He can also represent fear, but even when he is fearful, he never backs down in defense of himself or those he loves. He is also able to make leaps and bounds both literally and figuratively. Let's look at some of the other animals surrounding our Queen.

Owl~ The voice of secrets and the communicator between the ancient realms and present. Highly intuitive and protective.

Hummingbird~ Joy. Health. Healing. Magic. Simple pleasures. Endurance. A reminder that small things can bring immense joy.

Fish~ Abundance. Creativity. Unity. Dreams. Deeper wisdom. Secrets.

Snail~ Boundaries. Patience. Home. Patterns and cycles.

Butterfly~ Transformation. Surrender. Expansion.

Spider~ Femininity. Manifestation. Alchemy. Creativity. Intention.

Fairy/Faerie~ Magic. Nature. Balance. Light and dark.
You may also find yourself influenced or surrounded by someone characteristic of a queenly nature—a mother or mothering type of person.

Reversed~ Like the King, a reversed Queen showcases the more negative aspects of her character. Upright, the Queen can be nurturing and caring, while in reverse, she might be self-absorbed, fickle, authoritarian, or just plain mean. Again, remember even difficult personalities can teach us valuable lessons.

As mentioned above, Knights are doers. They have goals, and they get things done. While experienced, they are not as mature as Kings and Queens and can therefore lack control of their feelings, whereas the King and Queen have mastered theirs. *The Everglow* Knight is surrounded by five animals, representing movement within the suits. While the horse may charge into battle, he is an earthy animal reminding us of our need to remain grounded when tackling a situation. The turtle has the beautiful quality of existing both on land and in water, with a reminder not to let our emotions run away with us when handling situations. Sometimes it is best to take a slower, more methodical approach when dealing with a problem. The koi moves fluidly and does not fight the current; instead, it moves harmoniously from one place to another. The butterfly moves playfully through the air, with a reminder not to take life too seriously. And the seemingly tiny ladybug balances her fire and enthusiasm with the understanding that sometimes small steps produce the biggest results.

Horse~ Power. Movement. Grace. Nobility. Victory. Freedom.

Turtle~ Time. Patience. Groundedness. Longevity. Security.

Koi~ Prosperity. Relationships. Harmony.

Butterfly~ Transformation. Surrender. Secrets. Spirit.

Ladybug~ Passion. Luck. Protection.

Hint~ When the Knight shows up, you are being called to action. Look at the surrounding cards to determine what that action might entail. It is also possible you may find yourself involved with someone embodying the Knight's persona. Brothers and sisters may have influence at this time.

Reversed~ Because Knights are doers in the Court, anything reversed may be a negative aspect of the action. For example, it could be you are moving too fast or too slow in a situation—putting the cart before the horse. It could also suggest you are restless and bored. It could be you are lacking self-discipline. You could be overly emotional about a situation and need to take a deep breath before proceeding. If this pertains to a person, there could be a lot of illusory energy around them.

The Messenger represents the Page in the Tarot. Pages can represent younger people, even children. As people, they are full of energy at the beginning of their personal path. As a symbol, the Messenger is a catalyst for change. They arrive with messages about opportunities and new adventures. Our *Everglow* messenger is the beautiful stork. The stork represents creativity and prosperity. In folklore, the stork is the bringer of babies. How fitting that our stork would be here to deliver a message. He also has a companion—the dragonfly. How fitting, since Odonata, infraorder Anisoptera, has been around for millions of years. Symbolically they represent not only the higher realms, carrying ancient wisdom from Source, but also the subconscious realms, with messages from within.

Stork~ Birth. Creativity. Faith. Children. Messages.

Dragonfly~ Transformation. Wishes. Luck. Communication. Manifestation. Hope. Rebirth.

Hints~ When the stork appears, you are being provided a message. Change is afoot. Look at the surrounding cards to glean what those messages might mean.

Reversed~ Remember, the Messenger brings forth change. Any reversal will indicate a delay in some area, whether it be ideas, creativity, money, or communication.

THE ELEMENTALS

Elemental cards (Earth, Air, Fire, and Water) can be pulled with *The Everglow* Arcana or shuffled separately. When shuffled separately, they are a graphic card reference for *The Everglow* suit cards. If used with *The Everglow* Arcana cards, it is important to note that particular astrological signs may be influencing the situation. If multiple elemental cards appear, it is more likely to mean numerous signs are influencing the situation or that key aspects of the elemental's nature are essential. For example, an Air and Water card may indicate a need for balance between the head (Air) and the heart (Water). Also remember that certain elements don't mix, while others feed off each other. An example of not mixing would be Fire and Water, which could possibly mean conflict or a need for resolution. You could be putting out multiple fires. An example of feeding might be Air and Fire. Air feeds the Fire and could mean passion, energy, and drive. A project is moving forward quickly or taking off. It is important once again to look at the surrounding cards. If the cards surrounding Fire and Air appear negative, it could indicate gossip or a hot situation. Typically, though, it will suggest that whatever is happening will most likely burn hot but quickly resolve. Let's hope things don't get out of control! This is taking the element at face value. Some astrological signs interact very well together despite their elemental influence.

EARTH

AIR

FIRE

WATER

Here are the astrological signs connected to the elementals.

EARTH Taurus, Capricorn, Virgo

AIR Libra, Gemini, Aquarius

FIRE Aries, Leo, Sagittarius

WATER Scorpio, Pisces, Cancer

The elementals can also influence time frames, link to particular seasons, or provide more-profound meaning.

EARTH | WINTER
Time frame: A season to a year
Example: The project you initiated may take up to several months or even a year to complete. It may start or finish in the winter. It may involve something that is grounding or provides security.

AIR | FALL
Time frame: Weeks
Example: Those seeds you planted are starting to show some growth. Creative endeavors are beginning to take you somewhere.

FIRE | SPRING

Time frame: Days
Example: Sparks of inspiration. Lots of creative energy brewing. Whatever you initiate sees results within days.

WATER | SUMMER

Time frame: Months
Example: Take your time. Enjoy the moment. Nurture and go with the flow.
Sometimes, the elemental time frames play off each other. For example, Fire with Water may suggest that an idea will take a few months to show results. Depending on the cards surrounding them, these two cards might indicate a fiery and passionate relationship. It could also suggest a tumultuous one.

In general, the elemental cards mean the following:

Earth grounding energy, security, and foundations

Air thoughts, discernment, logic, ideas, and communication

Fire inspiration, creativity, sex, physical activity, and action

Water emotions, intuition, dreams, secrets, and the subconscious realms

the *EVERGLOW*
MINOR CARDS

The Everglow minor cards are based on themes within the traditional Tarot cards. Since *The Everglow* system does not contain separate suits like traditional Tarot, I decided to incorporate images that best represented overarching themes. However, these cards were not numbered, since I felt it would be a distraction to *The Everglow* majors. There are eighteen cards in total.

ABUNDANCE / LOSS

Many cultures see the pig as a symbol of good luck and fortune. Growing up, my family always had a pork roast on New Year's Day, in the hopes of abundance for the entire year. Of course, if you are a vegetarian, black-eyed peas are an excellent alternative.

How do you define abundance? Is it strictly a monetary thing? Abundance can come in many forms. Sometimes, we need an abundance of time or an abundance of rain. Creating abundance comes from our ability to receive and be in a state of gratitude. The ability to recognize and appreciate what you do have will attract more abundance to you. Be open to receiving. The upright position of this card is an indication of good fortune.

Reversed~ Loss comes to us all, but it is essential to remember that it is temporary. This too shall pass.

SYMBOL

Pig~ Abundance, wealth, prosperity, success, and resourcefulness

ADVERSITY / ADAPTATION

There are times when you will face instability and conflict. Not everyone will agree with you, and it's in those moments you will have to pick your battles wisely. Remember, every difficulty is an opportunity to learn. When someone rubs you the wrong way, or you feel agitated by a situation, it's the perfect moment to step back and examine "Why?" Adversity may feel uncomfortable, but it can be a great teacher.

Reversed~ You are making an effort to adapt to a difficult situation or see another's point of view. Conflict resolution is possible now. You are working together to solve problems. Others may appear different, but you realize you have more in common than you know.

SYMBOL

Seagull~ Adaptability, motivation, movement, communication, diversity (because there are many types), higher ground, view from above, waste not / want not, opportunity, resourcefulness, challenge, and resolution

ALTRUISM / EGOISM

You may be on a path of spiritual awakening that opens you up unselfishly to the needs of others. Setting ego aside, you see the oneness in others and that we are collectively connected and bound to one another beneath the surface. This is a great time to volunteer or provide your skills to help others in need. Perhaps you are surrounding yourself with or seeking out others who are altruistic.

Reversed~ You may have lost sight of the needs of others and become self-serving in your actions. Or, you find yourself involved with others or someone who does not have your best interest at heart.

SYMBOL

Buddha~ Love, compassion, wisdom, spirituality, growth, balance, peace, awakening, and serenity

BALANCE / IMBALANCE

The beauty of balance. When life is in balance, everything seems to fall into place and just flows. Am I right? Balance is achieved in many ways. There is a balance between masculine and feminine energies, between the heart and the head, in the give and take, yin and yang, cause and consequence, decisions and outcomes, etc. Balance occurs when there is flexibility and adaptability, and when we can make a choice through discernment. Sometimes, it is achieved through harmony.

Reversed~ When something is out of balance, something else will suffer. Often it is due to an inner struggle that needs clarification. Be careful of extremes.

SYMBOL

Cat~ Balance, alert, intuition, patience, independence, and relaxation

Rock~ Solid, grounded, stable, inflexibility, time, rootedness, strength, and foundational

COMPARE / CONTRAST

Mark Twain said, "Comparison is the thief of joy." Nothing could be more accurate. When I began many years ago as an artist, I would get very depressed seeing what other artists were creating, and wondered why I wasn't achieving equal success. I compared my work to others and constantly found fault within myself. This type of behavior kills the spirit. Each of us is unique and has talents, gifts, and abilities that are indeed our own. Take the time to concentrate on what makes you unique, and remember that this journey is your own. Cast aside any doubts so that you are open to receive. Be open to the differences of others. Be open to different perspectives.

Reversed~ "Be yourself. Everyone else is taken," said Oscar Wilde. Step out of your comfort zone and let your light shine. It's time to discover what sets you apart from others. Seek out individuals who are different and walk to the beat of their own drummer.

SYMBOL

Platypus~ Unique, comfortable, contradictions, and tolerance

CONFUSION / ORDER

The Octopus comes along when there is a need for flow and balance. You may be confused by too many choices or over-burdened by too much responsibility. Perhaps you feel as though you are being pulled in too many directions with little relief or guidance. Take a deep breath. Step back for some clarity. Make a to-do list. Get organized. Ask for help. We cannot be everything to everyone.

Furthermore, it is difficult to see clearly if we feel stressed and overwhelmed. Take a moment for yourself and breathe. Remember that if something is not working out or you con-tinually feel thwarted by your efforts, it might be time to change direction. Octopus is an adaptable creature with the ability to regenerate.

Reversed~ Now is the time for order before things get en-tirely out of control. Declutter or get organized. You will be surprised at how easily things flow and open up when you take control of what is controlling you. The other side of order is too much control. Be flexible and release the need to be overly controlling. Let others offer their gifts and services.

SYMBOL

Octopus~ Grounding, flow, adaptability, intuition, agility, flexibility, and regeneration

DISCIPLINE / TIME

Anything worth achieving takes hard work. Now is the time to apply discipline and focused attention to manifest your goals. They are within reach, and you are building new foundations in the process.

Reversed~ Everything in Divine timing. We live in an instant-gratification world, but sometimes what we want takes a bit more time and energy. Trust the process and know that when it is meant to be, it will manifest. Be open to receiving.

SYMBOL

Highland Cow~ Progress, stability, share the wealth, rootedness, earth, persistence, and blocks

DIVE DEEP / AVOIDANCE

Take some time to dive deep and listen. Something needs your attention. You may know what it is, or you may be struggling to figure it out. Either way, it is essential to go within and shine a light on what is hidden. It could be that old wounds are coming to the surface for healing, or old patterns need clearing.

Reversed~ Avoidance is any action that keeps you from dealing with something. It could be difficult people, emotions, or situations. While procrastinating, avoiding, or escaping may provide relief at the time, it's really a temporary fix to a deeper problem. When we don't face what is really troubling us, it can manifest as missed opportunities, further anxiety, or even illness. The first step in changing these behaviors is to recognize them as they occur. Journaling, meditation, therapy, and facing the things causing us to shrink are essential. It isn't always easy, but consistent recognition and being present is key. Anxiety is often rooted in our perceptions of the past or fear of the future. Is there something happening right now that is preventing you from moving forward? Can you think back to a time when you faced a similar situation? What emotions come to mind, and how would you change the outcome if you could?

SYMBOL

Fish~ Healing, emotions, intuition, subconscious, motives, mystery, rebirth, movement, flow, energy, abundance, courage, and tenacity

EXPANSION / DELAY

Seeds have been planted, and now it is time for expansion. Look out to the horizon and trust the process that everything is unfolding as it should. While you are still in the early stages of development, things are progressing. Creativity and research may be critical factors in moving things forward. You may be surrounding yourself with individuals who have something to bring to the table. You see significant growth in your efforts.

Reversed~ Delays occur for various reasons. It could be that you need to change direction, conduct more research, seek out help, or simply wait. Trust the process that a delay is for the best and highest good in a situation and that whatever is needed is forthcoming.

SYMBOLS

Sunflower~ Growth, vibrancy, joy, happiness, and vitality

Dragonfly~ Metamorphosis, transformation, emotions, joy, introspection, movement, illusions, and being present

HANG ON / LET GO

What are you hanging on to and why? Sometimes we hold so tightly to someone or something that we miss possible opportunities or relationships. I have often found this is due to fear. We think we will never find someone else or we can't possibly start over at this point in our lives. Remember, there is always time to change the road you're on.

Furthermore, you are worthy of change—positive change. Sometimes letting go leads you to something better, but you will never know unless you throw caution to the wind and release your grip. Letting go can be a form of forgiveness. Sometimes, it is releasing control. You don't have to be everything to everybody.

Reversed~ You are holding on too tightly and need to relinquish your fear of the unknown. Perhaps you have become too dependent on others and have therefore lost some of your identity. You are feeling overburdened and overwhelmed.

SYMBOLS

Panda~ Yin/yang, black and white, peace, strength, balance, comfort, security, healthful boundaries, nurture, and polarity

Tree~ Strength, steadfastness, growth, change, release, abundance, time, courage, and protection

HEAL / HARM

Whether you are recovering physically, emotionally, mentally, or spiritually, this card's purpose is to remind you of the importance of healing. Throughout your life, personally and collectively, events will test your resolve. Some will be easier than others, but ultimately healing will become an intrinsic part of the growth process. There is great knowledge on the other side of healing, and healing can be a choice. When this card shows up, it's asking you to examine what needs healing in your life. What do you need to remove from your life to heal? Is it food, toxic relationships, vices, or a job that no longer makes you happy? How can you help others heal? How can you help the planet heal? Remember that when one person suffers, it creates a ripple that affects others. The same can be said for healing. It is believed that when one person heals themselves, they are healing the ancestors of the past in their family line.

Reversed~ When the reverse of this card appears, it asks you to take a good long look at what may be causing you harm. Also, keep in mind that what we put out into the world, we receive in return. Do no harm—receive no harm.

SYMBOLS

Bear~ Bear medicine symbolizes awakening, courage, strength, taking care of self and family, enlightenment, and the spiritual journey. For Native Americans, the bear represents mysticism, magic, and healing.

PATIENCE / EXPECTANCY

They say good things come to those who wait. But the waiting can be difficult. We live in a world where much of what we want and need can be had at the push of a button. This has made us impatient and forgetful that sometimes things take time, especially when something is worthwhile. The old adage that everything happens in perfect Divine timing may be applied when this card appears. Remember delays are often blessings in disguise. Sometimes, when you get what you want, you may not want what you get. Sometimes no is the ultimate blessing.

Reverse~ Much like the upright message, the reversal of this card may indicate that you are overly expectant of specific results or in a rush to get things done. Rushing can cause imperfections to result, or if you are clinging too hard on an expectant outcome, the Universe cannot work its magic. Sometimes you need to let go of the how and just let things happen. You might be pleasantly surprised by the outcome.

SYMBOL

Snail~ Take your time, patience, enjoy the journey, release control, follow the path, slow down, caution, focus, and use your time wisely.

PEACE / GRATITUDE

In this image, our little squirrel is curled up in a comfy nest with his beloved nut. He's at peace and very happy with small gifts. Right outside his nest is an even larger nut, a symbol of gratitude in action.

Time to take a break and rest. Two things could be happening when this card makes an appearance. It could be you've been working very hard, and now it is time to ease back and enjoy the fruits of your labor. Or, it could be you are overworked and overburdened and need to physically rest. Take a break. Things will get done. Sometimes a needed break not only is enough to recharge your batteries but is also just what the doctor ordered to get your creative juices flowing. Remember, it is essential to take time to rest, or you may find you are forced to do so.

Reversed~ Gratitude is the first step in achieving abundance. Gratitude is energy. Sometimes it's difficult to feel grateful during a difficult situation. However, that is when it is most important to have perspective. Look around at what you do have to be grateful for, and you may find you have more than most. Remember, our little squirrel doesn't have much, but he's happy with what he does have. Gratitude is definitely an attitude.

SYMBOLS

Squirrel~ Abundance, multitasking, playfulness, preparedness, need to relax, and energy

PLAY / PLOD

I don't think there is anything cuter than watching baby goats play. Take some time to play and explore. Get out and socialize. Connect with others, belly-laugh, and dance like no one is watching.

Reversed~ You've become lost in the drudgery of work or life and, in doing so, have lost some inner spark. Perhaps you are consumed by the minutia of details. An imbalance has occurred. You may be taking on too much or taking things too seriously. If you feel overwhelmed and disconnected, take some time to examine what would make you feel happy.

SYMBOL

Goat~ Play, curiosity, vitality, sensuality, exploration, order, and stability

POTENTIAL / BLOCKS

The creation of a thousand forests is in one acorn.

~Ralph Waldo Emerson

The acorn is a seed similar to a chrysalis that remains dormant until it is ready to transform into the miraculous oak. Within its dormancy is tremendous growth potential. Potential is limitless. Now is the time to think big and be open to possibilities. Limit any negation in your thoughts and allow for the best to come your way. You are creating something beautiful.

Reversed~ Blocks have a purpose. However, we may not always understand why we feel blocked or why delays are occurring. Ultimately, a block or delay is an opportunity to readjust our plans, change course, or wait it out. Like Divine timing, sometimes a block is a speed bump leading you to greater potential.

SYMBOL

Acorn~ Prosperity, abundance, potential, luck, gift, and growth

SUCCESS / FAILURE

How do you feel about the word "success"? Does it make you think of abundance, or do you fear what may change should you reach a certain level of achievement? Success can be daunting because it opens doors to the unknown. However, now is your time to shine. Allow yourself to receive the accolades you deserve! Don't be afraid to step into the light and show your talent to others. Be proud of who you are. You have a great deal to offer.

Reversed~ Everyone fails from time to time. But failure is a great teacher. Many successful people have failed more times than they have been successful, and all will invariably say it was their failures that taught them to truly appreciate their successes. Failure is inevitable, but it doesn't mean you shouldn't try, nor does it mean you should assume that because you failed once, you will continue to do so. The right attitude can make all the difference.

SYMBOL

Peacock~ Self-expression, pride, dignity, leadership, integrity, attraction, and vision

According to the *Encyclopedia Britannica*, "symbiosis" is any of several living arrangements between members of two different species. In other words, they derive mutual benefit from one another by coinciding despite their differences. They use the example of the clown fish, which makes its home within a sea anemone. While the anemone will sting the clown fish, it also protects it from predators. In this card, I have used the gentle hummingbird. It is in its nature to live in harmony with its surroundings, seeking nectar to help in pollination, ultimately feeding other plants and the human species in return. They live in symbiotic harmony with one another. Symbiosis can undoubtedly have its disadvantages, but ultimately it is the coming together of two things to achieve either a good or ill goal. When this card appears, it may be asking you to look at the situation from another angle or open yourself up to something different that may produce a mutually satisfying result in the long run. Nothing in nature lives for itself. Be open to another way of doing things or another's point of view. There is a lot to learn from those who are different from us.

Reversed~ A lack of harmony is creating discord. Disagreements and differences of opinion are not unusual, but when they disrupt progress, it is time to examine the possibility of compromise. Are you or someone else being too rigid in your thinking? Are you allowing bias to cloud your ability to negotiate a peaceful and mutually satisfying outcome? Get to the heart of the matter.

SYMBOL

Hummingbird~ Small gifts, simple pleasures, endurance, perseverance, love, joy, luck, infinity, healing, and wisdom

Trust comes in many forms, but ultimately it is having faith without doubt in someone or something. Trust is formed when we feel seen and heard. Trust occurs when we feel secure. However, sometimes trust is challenging to achieve when it involves the unknown. We aren't sure of the result, so we fail to trust. This is often to our detriment when we place perceived notions on a possible outcome. I use the word "detriment" because when we negate a possibility by assuming it will not work out, the manifestation of our desires is lost. I can't recall where I heard this, but one of my favorite examples of this is ordering a meal in a restaurant. You place your order and do not question that it will appear on the table, how you ordered it, and in a reasonable amount of time. You just sit back and trust it will. Failure to trust is based on associated imprints from past experiences. Put those imprints and perceived fears aside and trust that what you want is on its way to you in the time that is needed for it to be perfect.

Reversed~ Fear is a four-letter word. Specifically, it can be said that fear stands for "**f**alse **e**vidence **a**ppearing **r**eal." We know the difference between real fear, such as being chased by a bad person, and perceived fear, which is the failure to trust on the basis of perceived outcomes. These perceptions are rooted in imprinting and trust issues. Now is a time to dive deep and examine why you are fearful. Fear can keep us from achieving desired goals. It can also keep things from manifesting in your life. Remember, "Everything you want is on the other side of fear" (Jack Canfield).

SYMBOL

Turtle~ Taking your time, wisdom, don't worry, trust, emotions, boundaries, safety, protection, grounding, determination, and longevity

the EVERGLOW
HOUSES

Most of us have read our daily horoscope. We may even be familiar with our moon and rising signs, but we may not be aware of how much astrology, and the astrological houses in particular, influence our lives. *The Everglow* wasn't created to give you a crash course in astrology. Oh my, this would be a much longer book if that were the case. However, as *The Everglow* began to take shape, I knew I wanted to include the astrological houses, because as the *Idiot's Guide to Astrology*, fourth edition, tells us, "The houses are the areas of your life experiences where the action is." Put it this way—while the Tarot may be the "why" something is happening, the twelve houses indicate "where" you are with that particular something and how it is influencing your life. Therefore, that is why the houses came to be a part of this deck. The house cards should be separated from all other cards, shuffled, and drawn separately. This will be explained in the chapter about reading the cards.

Each *Everglow* house card breaks down the major influences with a list of keywords.

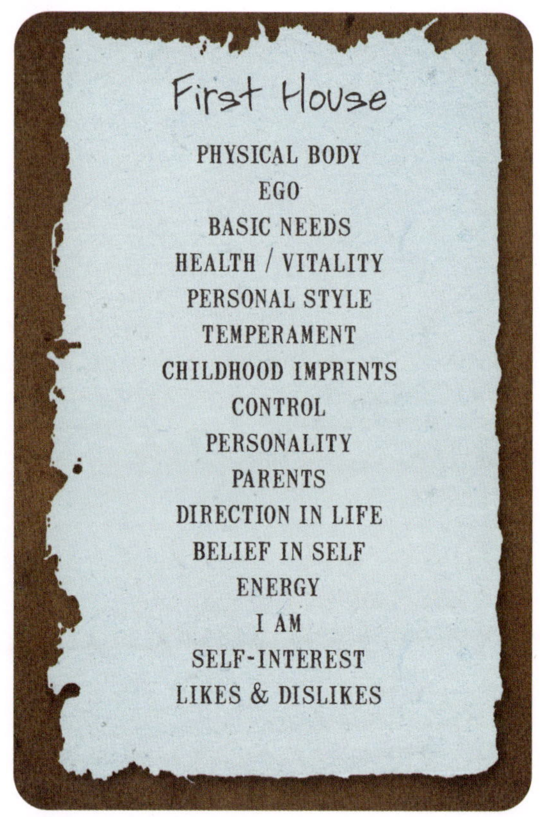

First House
PHYSICAL BODY
EGO
BASIC NEEDS
HEALTH / VITALITY
PERSONAL STYLE
TEMPERAMENT
CHILDHOOD IMPRINTS
CONTROL
PERSONALITY
PARENTS
DIRECTION IN LIFE
BELIEF IN SELF
ENERGY
I AM
SELF-INTEREST
LIKES & DISLIKES

In his work on the lost writings of *The Astrological Houses: The Spectrum of Individual Experiences*, Dane Rudhyar describes the first house as "the beginnings of human experience." This is where the personality is formed and awareness of self is created. It is the place where we test the waters of our existence. He further explains that the "first house is the realm of sheer awareness and of vision. In it, the individual is almost obsessed with potentiality, with happenings, with the sense of beginning, with the unformulatable urge to find the central truth and the foundation of his own personal being." This house is the physical self and where personality takes form.

Hint~ This is the house of manifestation through self-interest.

Ask yourself~ What do you want in life?

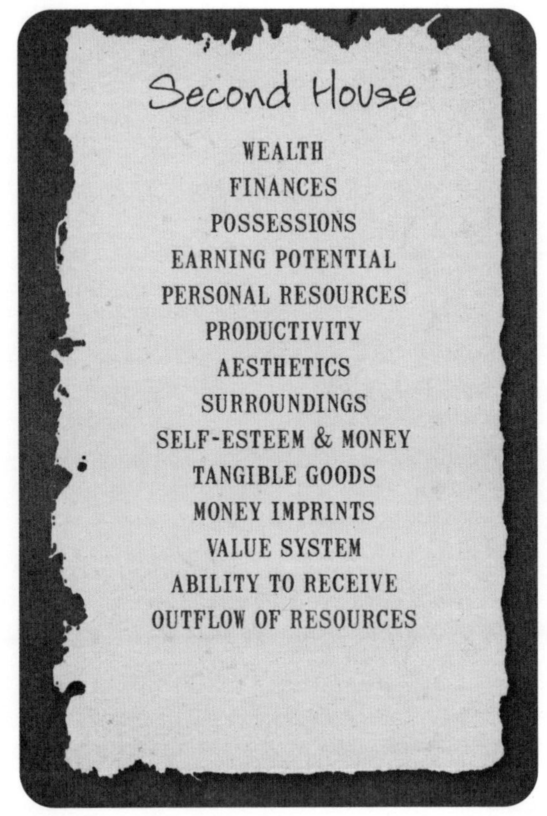

Second House

WEALTH
FINANCES
POSSESSIONS
EARNING POTENTIAL
PERSONAL RESOURCES
PRODUCTIVITY
AESTHETICS
SURROUNDINGS
SELF-ESTEEM & MONEY
TANGIBLE GOODS
MONEY IMPRINTS
VALUE SYSTEM
ABILITY TO RECEIVE
OUTFLOW OF RESOURCES

The second house is the "have" house and incorporates our wealth and tangible possessions. However, it isn't all about material gain. Much that is formed here also has to do with what we inherit in terms of personality, traits, gifts, and how we use them.

Hints~ Be aware of substituting material goods for self-worth.

Ask yourself~ What are your feelings surrounding abundance and wealth?

Do you feel you are worthy to receive abundance?

Do you feel that financial wealth is easy or difficult to achieve?

Are you letting financial wealth be a determining factor in who you are?

Are you afraid of what abundance might bring or change in your life?

Third House

ENVIRONMENT——WHERE YOU LIVE

COMMUNITY

NEIGHBORS

SIBLINGS

RESEARCH

PRIMARY EDUCATION

TRAVEL

COMMUNICATION——

WRITTEN & VERBAL

MEMORIES

PHYSICAL SKILLS

PERCEPTIONS

BIAS

LISTENING SKILLS

INTELLECTUAL PURSUITS

IMAGINATION

The third house consists of your interactions within various social environments and how they shape your personality. These would include where you live, neighbors, community, siblings, and education.

Hints~ Communication develops in this house, and therefore, if this card comes up, it is essential to examine how you communicate with yourself and others.

Be aware of those you attract in your life.

Difficult personalities are often teachers.

Listen to understand versus listening to respond.

Ask yourself~ What biases are affecting my perceptions?

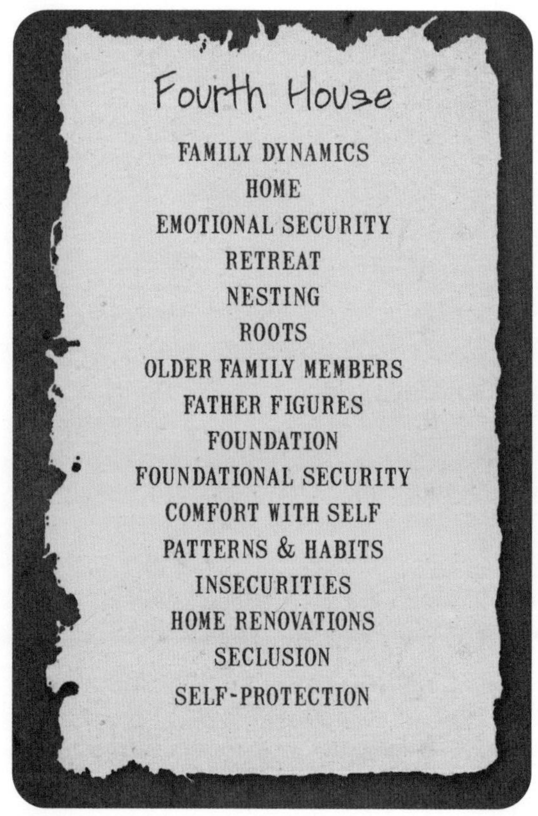
Fourth House
FAMILY DYNAMICS
HOME
EMOTIONAL SECURITY
RETREAT
NESTING
ROOTS
OLDER FAMILY MEMBERS
FATHER FIGURES
FOUNDATION
FOUNDATIONAL SECURITY
COMFORT WITH SELF
PATTERNS & HABITS
INSECURITIES
HOME RENOVATIONS
SECLUSION
SELF-PROTECTION

The fourth house, like the four in numerology, is about the home. This is where we build our sense of security, which typically begins in the home. But home is what we make of it—it is where we exist within our own skin. It is also the place where we tap into our emotional security or lack thereof. As I always say, think of the legs of a table. If you cut one of the legs off, the table will likely fall over. This is where we work on and repair our sense of security by examining our inner foundations.

Hints~ You may be examining your roots, ancestry, family values, and early imprints. You may be looking at where you live, how you live, and what makes you feel secure. Now may be a time of renovation both internally and externally.

You may make a physical move.

Parents may play a dominant role presently or in some subconscious way.

Ask yourself~ What does security mean to you?

What does the word "home" mean to you?

How can you bring a sense of both into your life?

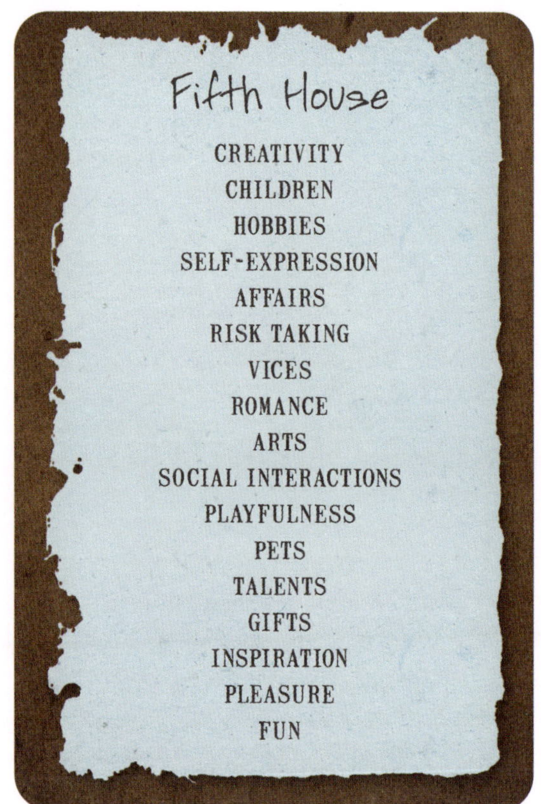
Fifth House
CREATIVITY
CHILDREN
HOBBIES
SELF-EXPRESSION
AFFAIRS
RISK TAKING
VICES
ROMANCE
ARTS
SOCIAL INTERACTIONS
PLAYFULNESS
PETS
TALENTS
GIFTS
INSPIRATION
PLEASURE
FUN

The fifth house is the house of creativity. But this doesn't just pertain to arts and crafts. This is our creative center, and from it flows our self-expression. It's also the house of pleasure, love, desire, vices, and risks. Here is where we examine why we are creative and how we express that to the outside world.

Hints~ This may be a highly creative time for you, and you may find that hobbies can be lucrative ventures.

You are expressing yourself through your passions.

Romance may be a factor.

Be careful not to indulge in risky behaviors as a means of creative outlet.

Ask yourself~ In what areas of your life are you taking healthful risks?

In what areas of your life are you taking unhealthful risks?

Do you feel you are expressing your true self?

How could you express more of who you are to the world?

Sixth House

HEALTH & WELL-BEING

SERVICE TO OTHERS

DAILY RESPONSIBILITIES

COWORKERS

JOB SATISFACTION

SKILLS

NUTRITION

TRUST & FEAR

COLLECTIVE CONSCIOUSNESS

SERVICE TO THE WORLD

PRIDE IN WORK

WORKPLACE COMMUNICATION

CAREER

Get to work! Responsibilities . . . everyone has them, and the sixth house is where you examine them. This is the "take care of yourself" house, the work and "daily grind" house. However, while you may be exploring how to better yourself, you may also be looking out for how you can be of service to others.

Hints~ Now may be a time when you are looking at how satisfied you are in your job or career.

Coworkers and interactions with them may play a dominant role in how you feel.

You may be examining your general health and diet and overall well-being.

You may be examining issues of trust, as well as fear-based thinking.

Be aware of imprints of the past, which may hinder your progress forward.

Now may also be a good time to be in service to others.

Ask yourself~ Are you happy with your job?

If not, what would you do if you could do anything?

What are your views on success and failure?

How can you help others?

What can you do to improve your overall health?

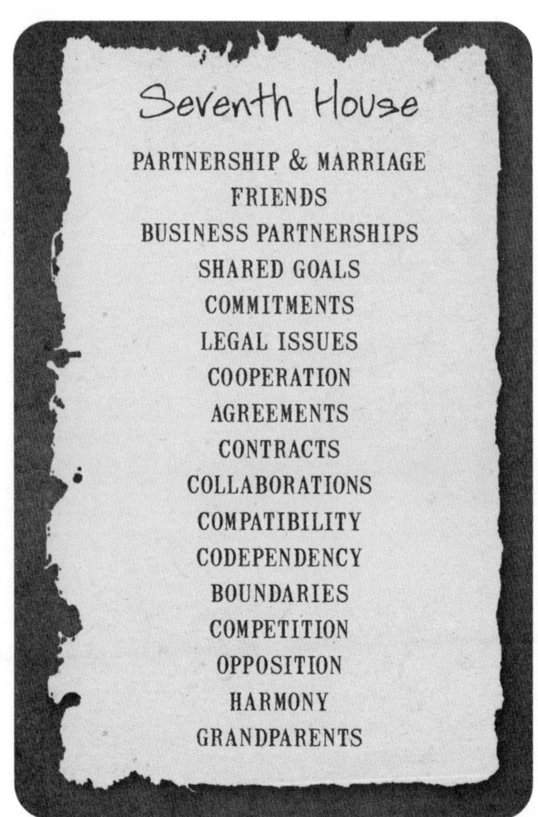

The seventh house, the house of partnership, is the realization of self through relationships. Unless you are entirely reclusive, you likely have many interactions daily and throughout your lifetime. Each exchange with the other, for better or worse, is a teacher in their own right.

In Rudhyar's book *The Astrological Houses: The Spectrum of Individual Experiences*, he states:

> Any relationship between equals must be based on the assumption that dynamic transformations of relationships are not only possible but necessary; for without them, there can be no individual growth and no really creative participation in the Whole. And there is no meaning to a relationship that does not lead the related individuals to experience their fullest possible participation in the life of society—in the "work of the world."

Hints~ Relationships of all kinds may factor heavily.

You may be examining your role, boundaries, codependencies, and shared goals.

This may also be a time where you are putting the needs of others ahead of your own. Marriage, romantic partnership, friendships, and business partnerships are just some of the types that have a significant impact now.

Cooperation and harmony are important.

Be aware of competitors or possible open enemies.

Legal contracts may be a factor.

Ask yourself~ Do you feel comfortable in your current relationships?

Is there anything you would like to change?

Eighth House

SHARED RESOURCES
(PARTNERS & OTHERS)
TAXES / INSURANCE
INHERITANCES
SEX
BIRTH / DEATH
AFTERLIFE
TRANSFORMATION (EMOTIONAL,
PHYSICAL & MENTAL)
REBIRTH
PSYCHIC ABILITIES
OCCULT MATTERS
SELF-IMPROVEMENT
MYSTERIES
INTENSE EMOTIONS
ESOTERIC THEMES
SPIRITUALISM

I like to refer to the eighth house as the house of death and taxes. It's where we examine things such as shared and financial resources and more-transformative issues such as birth, sex, and death.

Hints~ If this card comes up, you may be in the midst of profound change or exploring the deeper mysteries of life through the esoteric or spiritualism. Dreams and psychic awakenings may play a heavy role in your experiences.

Ask yourself~ What do you feel is missing from your life at the moment?

Have you been having prophetic dreams? It might be time to keep a dream journal.

Has anyone around you recently passed away?

Are you releasing places, people, or things that no longer serve your best and highest good?

How do you feel about these changes?

Ninth House

TEACHING
HIGHER EDUCATION
LAW
MARKETING
PUBLICATION
DISTANCE TRAVEL
BEHAVIORAL PATTERNS
FOREIGN MATTERS
FOREIGN CULTURES
PHILOSOPHICAL BELIEFS
SOCIAL CONSCIOUSNESS
RELIGION
A-HA! REVELATIONS
CULTURE
CUSTOMS

The ninth house involves travels of the mind and physical self. Educational endeavors, philosophy, expansions of the mind, beliefs, bias, and everything in between are important.

Hints~ You may be examining your inner world and how you project yourself in the outer world. Physical travel may also factor, as well as marketing and publication efforts, to reach a broader audience.

Ask yourself~ Are there any patterns that are keeping you from moving forward?

How do you think others see you?

Is it your most authentic self?

Are you masking or projecting a version of yourself to please others?

Tenth House

REPUTATION
CAREER ASPIRATIONS
SOCIAL STANDING
AMBITIONS
PERSONAL POWER
LEADERSHIP ABILITIES
ABILITY TO INSPIRE
DETERMINATION
INDIVIDUALITY
WORK / LIFE BALANCE
PUBLIC PERSONAL
PROFESSION
SUCCESS THROUGH EFFORTS
ACHIEVEMENTS

The tenth house is the house of reputation and career aspirations. Ambitions, dreams, and goals are essential, as is your public persona.

Hints~ You may be taking on a leadership role, exploring your personal power, or others may be taking note of your ability to inspire. Personal magnetism plays an important role in your success. Work/life balance may factor heavily at this time, and it is essential not to put ambitions before others.

Ask yourself~ Are you pursuing success at the cost of others?

Is the pursuit making you happy or filling an emotional need?

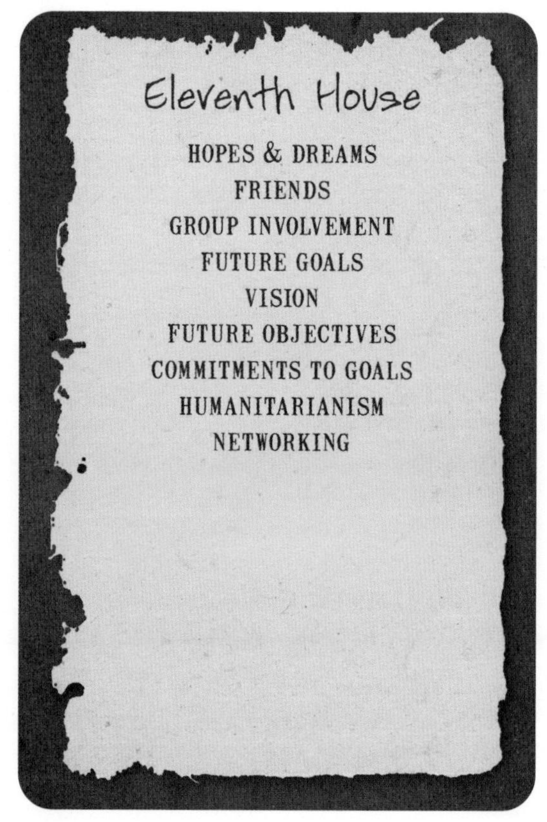

Eleventh House

HOPES & DREAMS
FRIENDS
GROUP INVOLVEMENT
FUTURE GOALS
VISION
FUTURE OBJECTIVES
COMMITMENTS TO GOALS
HUMANITARIANISM
NETWORKING

The eleventh house encompasses your hopes, dreams, and wishes. It's the social house where your interactions are likely to help drive your future endeavors.

Hints~ You may be connecting with like-minded individuals and working toward a common goal.

You may be thinking of the bigger picture, and service to others may be important to you.

You are future driven and dreaming big.

Planning and networking are important and a great way to connect with others who can further your goals.

Ask yourself~ Are there any groups or communities you can join that would help you achieve your goals?

What actions or measures are you taking to move yourself toward your goals?

Twelfth House

SECRETS
SUBCONSCIOUS MIND
MYSTICISM
SKELETONS IN THE CLOSET
WORKING BEHIND THE SCENES
SPIRITUAL RETREAT
SECLUSION
HEIGHTENED INTUITION
INNER CALLING
HIGHER PURPOSE
HEALING & CLEARING
BREAKING PATTERNS
THE PAST
TRANSCENDING EGO
NEED FOR PEACE
INNER LIFE REFLECTION
EXPLORING THE UNKNOWN

The twelfth house has its challenges, but it is because it's so mysterious. It involves secrets, the subconscious mind, and all the things coming up to the surface that need healing. It is where ego and soul connect to discover the Divine.

Hints~ You may be in the midst of inner transformation.

You may find comfort in retreat, to do some soul searching.

You may find a strong connection to your inner calling and higher purpose.

Working from home may be beneficial.

You may be experiencing a heightened sense of awareness.

Patterns and imprints from the past may be resurfacing for healing and clearing.

Ask yourself~ Are you experiencing any synchronicities?

Is anything coming up to the surface emotionally that needs clearing?

Why do you think it is appearing now?

Numbers, numbers, numbers.

You see them everywhere. And I can bet you see repeat numbers daily such as 333, 444, and 555. I'm continually pointing them out and taking note of the significance of numbers. Before we placed a bid on our home, I had to look up the symbolism behind the house number. Luckily, the number indicated that the house had chosen us—significant because it felt like a big hug when we entered.

One of the best books I have ever read on the subject of numerology is *Numerology: Key to the Tarot* by Sandor Konraad. In it, he connects numerology with the Tarot, which is the best way to learn the Tarot, in my opinion. He also goes into further detail about how numbers relate to astrology, personality, and just about anything else you can think of. In his book, he explains that the first nine numbers are root numbers, which incorporate all the numbers in the world. Compound numbers, when broken down to a single digit, become a root number. This is important because each root number is rich in symbolism. He explains that ten is the "bridge" between the roots and compound numbers. I have included the number zero in *The Everglow* deck. While it is traditionally not part of the Tarot's Minor Arcana and appears as the Fool card only in the Major Arcana, I felt zero needed a bigger role, and that is why it is part of this deck.

For the purpose of this deck, I drew specifically on numerology's relationship to the Tarot. In traditional Tarot, there are ten cards within each suit after the court cards, representing something significant in numerology. For *The Everglow*, I have used cards 1 through 10 but also added zero for a total of eleven number cards. No matter what suit you are dealing with, each number indicates the same set of keywords, but the influence may be different depending on the suit itself. For example, the number 1 indicates seeds being planted. This is true whether you are talking about cups, rods, swords, or coins. *The Everglow* puts these suits in four separate cards—Emotions (Water/Cups), Action (Fire/Rods), Thoughts (Air/Swords), and Security (Earth/Coins). However, the influence of one changes depending on the suit, as suggested above. For example, seeds being planted with the number 1 and paired with Air/Swords/Thoughts may indicate ideas. Water/Cups/Emotions may reveal feelings around those seeds being planted. Fire/Rods/Action might focus on the initial steps that one needs to take. And Earth/Coins/Security may require initial funds to get a project off the ground. Of course, there is more significance to the number 1 than just seeds being planted. Each number card in *The Everglow* has a list of keywords connected to that number in the Tarot.

*Hints~*When laying out a spread, add up the numbers on the cards and break them down to a root number. Then, find the corresponding number card and see if it provides you with further food for thought. Below is each of *The Everglow*'s number cards and the keywords as they relate to the Tarot.

ZERO

Ask yourself~ What would you do if you could do anything?

What patterns are repeating?

ONE

Ask yourself~ Where is there opportunity for growth?

What areas of your life need seeding, toiling, or rebuilding?

TWO

Ask yourself~ Where can you achieve balance and harmony in your current relationships?

What areas need flexibility?

Is there mutual give and take to your current relationships?

If not, how can this balance be restored?

THREE

Ask yourself~ Would further education or research be beneficial right now?

Would working in a group or community be helpful?

6
CYCLES
POTENTIALITY
FREEDOM

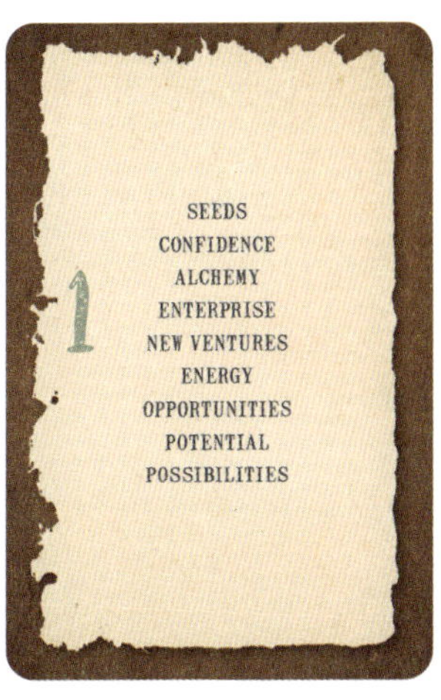

1
SEEDS
CONFIDENCE
ALCHEMY
ENTERPRISE
NEW VENTURES
ENERGY
OPPORTUNITIES
POTENTIAL
POSSIBILITIES

2
BALANCE
MODERATION
DEVELOPMENT
DUALITY
RELATIONSHIP
PARTNERSHIP
EYE TO EYE
OPPOSITES
COMPARISONS
DECISIONS / CHOICES
DIRECTION / PATH
COOPERATION / DIPLOMACY
PATIENCE
METHODIC APPROACH
HARMONY
FLEXIBILITY

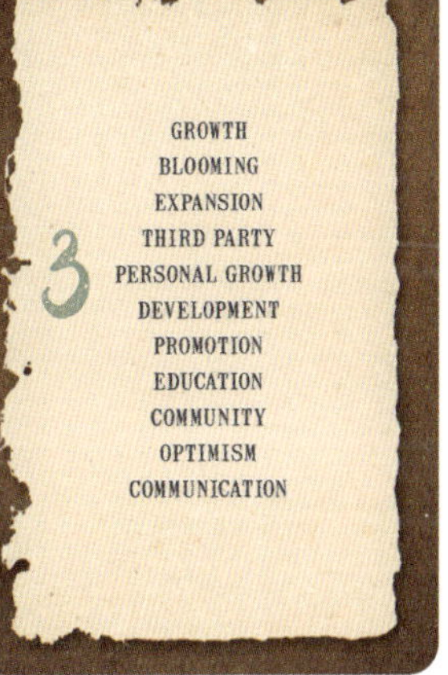

3
GROWTH
BLOOMING
EXPANSION
THIRD PARTY
PERSONAL GROWTH
DEVELOPMENT
PROMOTION
EDUCATION
COMMUNITY
OPTIMISM
COMMUNICATION

FOUR

Ask yourself~ In what ways are you seeking security or building stronger foundations?

What areas need stronger foundations and security?

FIVE

Ask yourself~ What challenges are you currently facing?

How might these challenges expand your personal growth?

SIX

Ask yourself~ Reflect back to a time when things were out of balance and how you were able to restore equilibrium. Could anything you learned be applied to a current situation that is out of balance?

SEVEN

Ask yourself~ What are some of the ways you are showing up in your life?

How might setting personal boundaries be beneficial to self-growth?

4

FOUNDATIONS
GROUNDING
SECURITY
HARD WORK
STRUCTURE
STABILITY
CONTROL
MANAGEMENT
RELIABILITY
PRACTICALITY
DISCIPLINE
ORGANIZATION

Sometimes involves authority figures or family members

5

IMBALANCE
ADJUSTMENT
COMPETITION
RESOURCEFULNESS
CHALLENGES
CHANGE
INSTABILITY
POSSIBLE TRAVEL
RELOCATION
RISKS
DISRUPTION
RESTLESS ENERGY
FLUCTUATIONS
NEW OPPORTUNITIES

Sometimes involves family or career dynamics

6

EQUILIBRIUM
RESTORED BALANCE
RECOGNITION
REWARD
HARMONIOUS ENERGY
REFLECTION
FAMILY / RELATIONSHIP
DOMESTIC OBLIGATIONS
CALM AFTER STORM

7

CHOICE
TRAVEL POSSIBILITIES
RESEARCH
REEVALUATION
SELF-DISCOVERY
BOUNDARIES
INNER GROWTH
AUTHENTICITY
TURNING POINT
INTROSPECTION
MEDITATION
SPIRITUALITY

EIGHT

Ask yourself~ How do you define success?

How are you stepping into your power?

What changes or transitions are you currently experiencing, and are they forcing you out of your comfort zone?

NINE

Ask yourself~ Are you experiencing any epiphanies, synchronicities, or prophetic dream messages?

What communication is coming through and how does it make you feel?

Can you relate it to anything from the past that needs healing?

TEN

Ask yourself~ What is coming to completion?

What is opening up for you?

How does the ending or beginning of something new make you feel?

Does it bring up any fears or concerns?

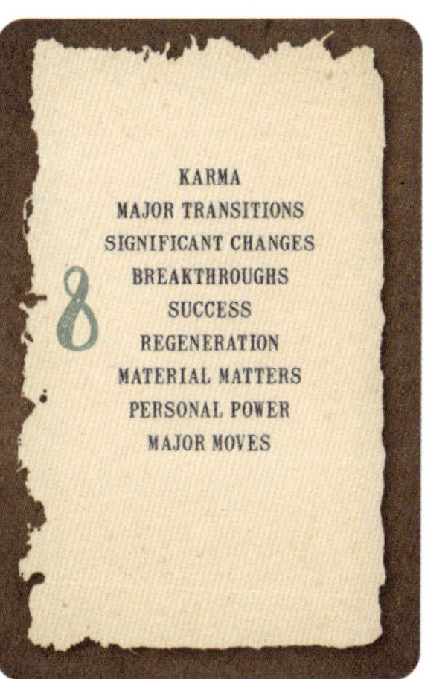

8
KARMA
MAJOR TRANSITIONS
SIGNIFICANT CHANGES
BREAKTHROUGHS
SUCCESS
REGENERATION
MATERIAL MATTERS
PERSONAL POWER
MAJOR MOVES

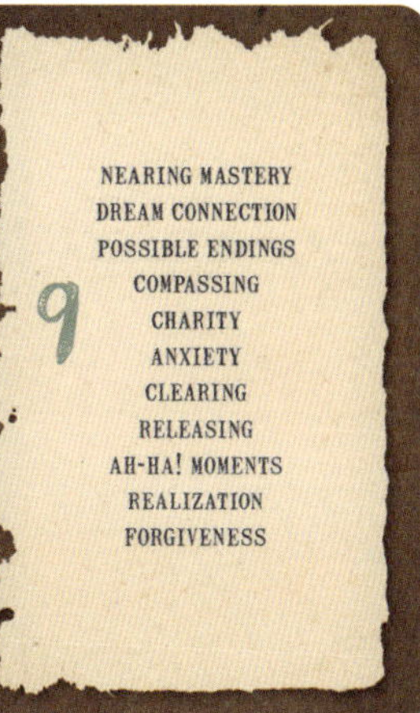

9
NEARING MASTERY
DREAM CONNECTION
POSSIBLE ENDINGS
COMPASSING
CHARITY
ANXIETY
CLEARING
RELEASING
AH-HA! MOMENTS
REALIZATION
FORGIVENESS

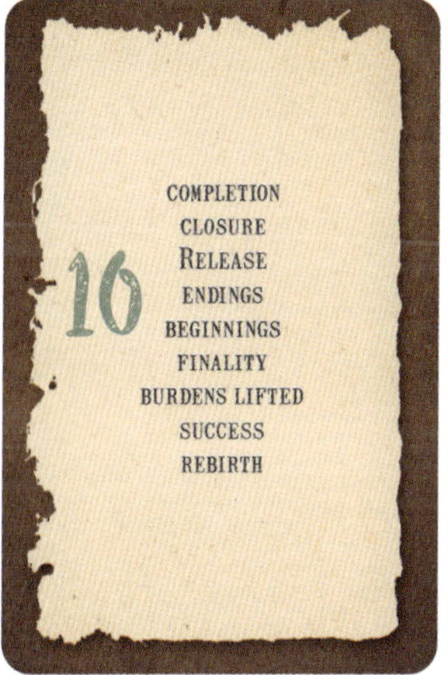

10
COMPLETION
CLOSURE
RELEASE
ENDINGS
BEGINNINGS
FINALITY
BURDENS LIFTED
SUCCESS
REBIRTH

the EVERGLOW
SUIT CARDS

The Everglow suit cards are similar to the elemental cards, but instead of the elemental cards' visual image, the suit cards provide more detail about how they are related to that particular suit. In traditional Tarot, the suits would be separated into Cups/Emotions, Swords/Thoughts, Coins/Security, and Wands/Action. Within those suits, you would have ten individual cards along with your court cards. There is no need for this in *The Everglow*. They work similarly with just four cards and may be drawn in a variety of ways (see example draws).

Action

PRIMAL ENERGY
MOTIVATION / CREATIVITY
ENTHUSIASM / EXCITEMENT
SEXUALITY / CAREER

ELEMENT: FIRE
SEASON: SPRING
TIME FRAME: DAYS

SIGNS
ARIES / LEO / SAGITTARIUS

PERSONALITY
ENERGETIC / CHARISMATIC

NEGATIVE TRAITS
LAZINESS / ARROGANCE
IMPULSIVITY

Emotions

FEELINGS / RELATIONSHIPS
ARTISTIC ENDEAVORS
IMAGINATION / INTUITION
SELF-LOVE / OTHERS' NEEDS
DREAMS / WOUNDED HEALER

ELEMENT: WATER
SEASON: SUMMER
TIME FRAME: MONTHS

SIGNS
SCORPIO / PISCES / CANCER

PERSONALITY
ARTISTIC / NURTURING

NEGATIVE TRAITS
OVERLY EMOTIONAL / FEARFUL
NEEDY

Security

SEX / EGO / WORK / HEALTH
FINANCES / FOUNDATION
STRUCTURE / BASIC NEEDS
TANGIBLE ITEMS / PHYSICAL WORLD

ELEMENT: EARTH
SEASON: WINTER
TIME FRAME: A SEASON TO A YEAR

SIGNS
TAURUS / VIRGO / CAPRICORN

PERSONALITY
ORGANIZED & PRACTICAL

NEGATIVE TRAITS
MATERIALISTIC / OVERINDULGENT
POSSESSIVE

Thoughts

INTELLECT / DISCERNMENT
LOGIC / COMMUNICATION / SERIOUS
ANALYTICAL / TRUTH SEEKER

ELEMENT: AIR
SEASON: FALL
TIME FRAME: WEEKS

SIGNS
LIBRA / GEMINI / AQUARIUS

PERSONALITY
FAIR / OPEN-MINDED
EXCELLENT LEADERS

NEGATIVE TRAITS
INSENSITIVITY / HEAD OVER HEART
INDECISIVENESS / CONFUSION
WORRIES / DETACHMENT

THE TIME FRAME CARDS

Einstein, when describing the passing of a friend, wrote, "That signifies nothing. For us believing physicists, the distinction between past, present, and future is only a stubbornly persistent illusion." He went on to prove this with his masterpiece, the general theory of relativity. If time is an illusion, then it may be safe to say that our perception of events in time, which is primarily based on imprints from the past, may be an illusion as well. And while Einstein's theory may prove that time is relative, I think that many of us can agree as spiritual beings experiencing a human experience that we often find our future thoughts are actually impressions of the past guiding us. We are rarely present. Is this because the present is an illusion of our making? While I am not a physicist, only a general observer, this has led me to understand that life is a series of patterns based on things we originally learned and observed; therefore, we cannot move forward until we have dealt with the past. Ergo, we can achieve this only if we are present.

The idea of time has always fascinated me, and as humans, we are obsessed with it, continually wondering when something will happen or when we will meet our soulmate. As a matter of fact, that last question is perhaps the most sought-after answer in the Tarot. However, I feel like nothing futuristic can occur if we are not in complete understanding of WHO we are, and this involves how we see ourselves through time.

Time frame cards are used in conjunction with the spreads that follow. To pick a time frame card when used with a spread, simply shuffle and draw a card.

The Future

THE FUTURE IS ALWAYS IN MOTION.
YOU HAVE FREE WILL.
QUESTIONS TO ASK YOURSELF:

What is my perception of
the possible outcome?
Will this make me feel good or bad?
What doors will this open or close?
What will this change?
What will remain the same?
Will this bring closure or healing
to a particular situation?
What do I need to be aware of?
What do I hope will happen?
What do I think could go wrong?

The Past

INFLUENCES FROM THE PAST MAY
INCLUDE THE FOLLOWING:

DNA / Pain / Bias
Fear / Choices / Teachers
Ancestry / Nostalgia / Religion
Education / Environment
Living situation / Parental imprints
Past relationships
Previous outcomes

The Present

HOW TO DETERMINE IF YOU ARE
BEING PRESENT.
QUESTIONS TO ASK YOURSELF:

Am I avoiding others?
Am I avoiding anything?
Where do I feel this in my body?
What message is this feeling
trying to convey?
How does this situation make
me feel in general?
Am I making excuses?
Am I shifting blame or responsibility?
Am I looking to be fixed,
saved, or rescued?
Am I repeating old patterns?
Is my emotional state interfering
with my discernment?
Am I being authentic?

What do I need to know about?

HOME / FAMILY
CHILDREN / CAREER
EDUCATION / CREATIVITY
TRAVEL / HEALTH / DIRECTION
SOUL PATH / SPIRITUALITY
COMMUNITY / WORLD
FRIENDSHIP / LOVE
CHALLENGES / PATTERNS
LIVING ENVIROMENTS

the EVERGLOW
SAMPLE SPREADS

Hint~ With all *The Everglow* spreads, don't forget to look into the animal symbolism and how it resonates with the question.

SUIT SPREAD

If you want to draw strictly from the suit cards, place them in a separate, shuffled pile. Your image cards (majors, minors, elementals, and court cards) should also be in a separate, shuffled pile. Focus on your question. Draw an image card and then pull a card from the separate suit pile to see the situation's suit. You can also lay out each suit (Emotions, Security, Thoughts, and Actions) and pull an individual image card to determine each situation's underlying message (example below).

In the first example, the querent wanted to switch jobs but wasn't sure if she should at this time. She pulled the Action card from the suits and the major card 15 Shadow/Confrontation (equivalent to the Devil). Action appears wise, but it would seem something is holding her back from moving forward. This would be a good time to journal some of the fears she has about leaving her old job for a new one.

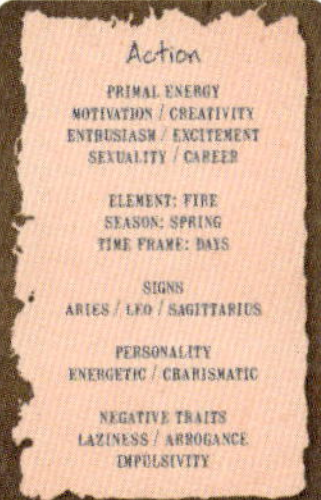

In the second example, utilizing the same question, we see a broader, more in-depth reading. When a card is drawn under each suit, it emphasizes areas within the suit that may need examining. Altogether, these cards form a bigger picture. The Abundance/Self-Care card, equivalent to the Empress in the Tarot, may reflect the need to examine past imprint issues around lack or abundance and the possible need to release self-limiting thoughts and behaviors, as evidenced by the next card. In reverse, the number 20 card is equivalent to the Judgment card in the Tarot and would indicate that she is shrinking from a path that might provide much-needed growth. It might be a good time to examine emotions around success and failure. What will change if she rises to the occasion and walks the path? Are there areas keeping her restricted, as evidenced by the Shadow/Confrontation card in reverse? Perhaps it goes back to security or playing safe. Is self-talk or imposter syndrome playing a part in moving forward? What self-limiting beliefs need releasing? This would be a great time to examine all of these things to determine what may be

holding her back from moving forward. The beauty is that the number 3 card in the upright indicates abundance, and stronger foundations are possible if she can confront some of the shadow issues that may keep her in patterns that prevent her from moving forward. It is important to remember that we all are deserving of abundance. Believing she is worthy of receiving is half the battle.

TIME FRAME SPREAD—PAST, PRESENT, AND FUTURE CARDS

The Everglow time frame cards (past/present/future) help determine where you are focusing your attention in a specific situation. They should be separated from all other cards, shuffled facedown, and then drawn. Typically, only one card is removed from the pile. However, you can also turn all three cards faceup in order of past, present, and future and then ask a specific question about each card by drawing from The Everglow image cards.

Here is an example of a Past, Present, and Future spread with *The Everglow* image cards. In this situation, the querent was having difficulty with a particular book project and wanted to know what was holding her back.

The past indicates something that involved fear. My question to her would be to look at specific situations in the past where fear played a factor. Was it fear of failure? Did she fail at something she wanted? Remember, failure is an opportunity for growth. Therefore, what did she learn from that situation? In the present, she may need to seek advice or guidance, or even some inner reflection would be beneficial. Perhaps more education is necessary, or a partnership might help. The future position shows us a chrysalis, reminding us that deep, transformative work is happening beneath the surface. Perhaps coming to terms with past fears and seeking guidance will help transform her future endeavors.

I would also suggest adding up the numbers on the cards and reducing them to a single digit to glean further insight from numerology cards. In this situation, the numerology card would be an 8. I would then ask her to reflect upon the keywords for the number 8 and how they make her feel in the situation regarding the past, present, and future (example below).

DAILY DRAW

The beauty of *The Everglow* is that while similar to the Tarot, it can also be used as an oracle. One of those ways is through a daily draw. For this, you would use only the image cards from *The Everglow*. Meditate on your question. I always find that the best answers occur when the querent asks, "What do I need to know about …?" Or you can simply ask, "What do I most need to know today?" You can try asking about subjects such as home, family, career, or health. Shuffle the cards and place them facedown. Draw one card to see what the universe wants you to be aware of today.

When you turn the card over, ask yourself how the image makes you feel. How do you feel about the words? Is the card upright or reversed?

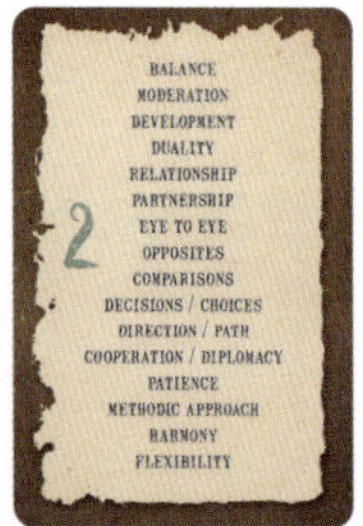

NUMEROLOGY SPREAD

Shuffle your number cards and place them facedown. You can use the number cards by themselves or pull an image card to pair with the number card for more in-depth reading. Focus on your question and pull your cards. In this situation, the querent was concerned about writing a novel. She pulled the Manifestation card in the upright position and the number 2. We deduced that she clearly had skills due to the manifestation card, but the 2 indicated that she was at the beginning phase of her work. Perhaps more research would be required, or she needed to think about work/life balance. Did she have time set aside to dedicate to writing her book?

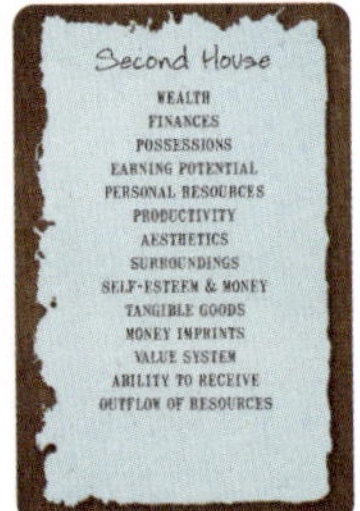

ASTROLOGY SPREAD

For the Astrology draw, separate the shuffled image cards from the house cards. Focus on your question and then pull a card from each pile. The house card will indicate what area is being affected by the issue. In this example, we used the same querent's question about switching jobs as we did in the Suit spread. In this spread, the Manifestation/Focus (Magician) card and the Second House card were drawn. If you remember, the second house is known as the "have" house and pertains to our material goods. Paired with the Manifestation card, it would seem that her focus in switching jobs may be on achieving or maintaining material wealth. Remember the spider symbolism. The spider utilizes everything within to create what it wants, and it does so with skill. This may be when she needs to put her skills to use to manifest the world she wishes to create.

the EVERGLOW
SPREAD

Now we have arrived at *the Everglow* spread, which is my favorite because it provides so much information. The first thing you want to do is make individual piles for your shuffled image, numerology, house, time frame, and suit cards. You can choose to leave the court and elemental image cards with the other picture cards or put them in separate piles. It's a matter of choice. If you decide to leave the elemental cards in, remember that certain astrological signs may be influencing the situation, or critical aspects of the elemental's nature are influencing the situation. Once you are grounded and centered, focus on your question and pull a card from each pile. You can draw more than one image card if you wish, but I find that one is typically all that is needed. The querent wanted to know what was influencing her current partnership. In this situation, she has pulled the Balance/Imbalance card in the reversed position along with the numerology card 2, Emotions suit, seventh house, and the Present card. For the querent, she realized much of the issue surrounded a give-and-take situation in her relationship. Things were out of balance between her and her partner. She spent some time journaling her thoughts and later pulled more cards for advice on the situation. What do you think is happening?

BALANCE / IMBALANCE

2

BALANCE
MODERATION
DEVELOPMENT
DUALITY
RELATIONSHIP
PARTNERSHIP
EYE TO EYE
OPPOSITES
COMPARISONS
DECISIONS / CHOICES
DIRECTION / PATH
COOPERATION / DIPLOMACY
PATIENCE
METHODIC APPROACH
HARMONY
FLEXIBILITY

Emotions

FEELINGS / RELATIONSHIPS
ARTISTIC ENDEAVORS
IMAGINATION / INTUITION
SELF-LOVE / OTHERS' NEEDS
DREAMS / WOUNDED HEALER

ELEMENT: WATER
SEASON: SUMMER
TIME FRAME: MONTHS

SIGNS
SCORPIO / PISCES / CANCER

PERSONALITY
ARTISTIC / NURTURING

NEGATIVE TRAITS
OVERLY EMOTIONAL / FEARFUL
NEEDY

Seventh House

PARTNERSHIP & MARRIAGE
FRIENDS
BUSINESS PARTNERSHIPS
SHARED GOALS
COMMITMENTS
LEGAL ISSUES
COOPERATION
AGREEMENTS
CONTRACTS
COLLABORATIONS
COMPATIBILITY
CODEPENDENCY
BOUNDARIES
COMPETITION
OPPOSITION
HARMONY
GRANDPARENTS

The Present

HOW TO DETERMINE IF YOU ARE
BEING PRESENT.
QUESTIONS TO ASK YOURSELF:

Am I avoiding others?
Am I avoiding anything?
Where do I feel this in my body?
What message is this feeling
trying to convey?
How does this situation make
me feel in general?
Am I making excuses?
Am I shifting blame or responsibility?
Am I looking to be fixed,
saved, or rescued?
Am I repeating old patterns?
Is my emotional state interfering
with my discernment?
Am I being authentic?

BIBLIOGRAPHY

Web Sources~

Einstein quote: https://www.quantamagazine.
org/a-debate-over-the-physics-of-time-20160719/
https://www.ancient-symbols.com/
https://www.auntyflo.com/magic/oyster
https://www.britannica.com/art/mask-face-covering/The-wearing-
  of-masks
https://www.britannica.com/science/symbiosis
https://www.buildingbeautifulsouls.com/symbols-meanings/five-ele-
  ments-symbolic-meaning/fire-element-symbolic-meaning/
https://www.drbeckybeaton.com/
https://www.gemsociety.org/article/history-legend-pearls-gems-yore/
https://www.nanticokeindians.org/page/tale-of-two-wolves
https://www.psychologytoday.com/us/blog/light-and-shadow/201302/
  gifts-the-shadow
https://www.spirit-animals.com/
https://www.spirit-animals.com/panda-symbolism/
https://urnabios.com/pine-tree-symbolism
https://www.whats-your-sign.com/
https://www.wizardingworld.com/
https://www.worldbirds.org/
https://www.zengyotaku.com/carp_jump_dragon_gate.html